30
CONVERSATIONS
EVERY MOM
Must Hav
TEENAGE

The quoted ideas expressed in this book (but not Scripture verses) are not, in all cases, exact quotations, as some have been edited for clarity and brevity. In all cases, the author has attempted to maintain the speaker's original intent. In some cases, quoted material for this book was obtained from secondary sources, primarily print media. While every effort was made to ensure the accuracy of these sources, the accuracy cannot be guaranteed. For additions, deletions, corrections, or clarifications in future editions of this text, please write Freeman-Smith.

Scripture quotations are taken from:

The Holy Bible, King James Version (KJV)

The Holy Bible, New International Version (NIV) Copyright © 1973, 1978, 1984, by International Bible Society. Used by permission of Zondervan Publishing House. All rights reserved.

The Holy Bible, New King James Version (NKJV) Copyright © 1982 by Thomas Nelson, Inc. Used by permission.

Holy Bible, New Living Translation, (NLT) copyright © 1996. Used by permission of Tyndale House Publishers, Inc., Wheaton, Illinois 60189. All rights reserved.

The Message (MSG)- This edition issued by contractual arrangement with NavPress, a division of The Navigators, U.S.A. Originally published by NavPress in English as THE MESSAGE: The Bible in Contemporary Language copyright 2002-2003 by Eugene Peterson. All rights reserved.

New Century Version®. (NCV) Copyright © 1987, 1988, 1991 by Word Publishing, a division of Thomas Nelson, Inc. All rights reserved. Used by permission.

The New American Standard Bible®, (NASB) Copyright © 1960, 1962, 1963, 1968, 1971, 1972, 1973, 1975, 1977, 1995 by The Lockman Foundation. Used by permission.

The Holman Christian Standard Bible™ (HCSB) Copyright © 1999, 2000, 2001 by Holman Bible Publishers. Used by permission.

Cover Design by Kim Russell / Wahoo Designs
Page Layout by Bart Dawson

ISBN 978-1-60587-340-4

Printed in the United States of America

30 CONVERSATIONS EVERY MOM

Must Have with Her
TEENAGE DAUGHTER

Introduction
A MESSAGE TO MOMS

B ecause you're older and wiser than your daughter, you have much to teach her (even if she doesn't think so). But what lessons should you teach first? After all, you probably have hundreds of ideas rattling around in your brain, all of them important. And with so many things to consider, you may find it tough to organize your thoughts. So, perhaps you haven't yet taken the time to sit down with your daughter and share your own personalized set of life-lessons in a systematic way. If that's the case, this book can help.

This text focuses on 30 timeless insights for Christians, lessons that your daughter desperately needs to hear from you. So here's your assignment: read this book, add your own personal insights, and then schedule a series of face-to-face, no-interruptions-allowed, parent-to-girl talks with the young woman whom God has entrusted to your care. Carve out enough time to really explore these concepts, and don't be afraid to share your own personal experiences: your victories, your defeats, and the lessons you learned along the way.

We live in a world where far too many parents have out-sourced the job of raising their kids, with predictably sour results. And make no mistake, your daughter is going to learn about life from somebody; in fact, she's learning about life every single day—some of the lessons are positive, and quite a few aren't. So ask yourself: Is your child being tutored by the world or by you? The world will, at times, intentionally mislead her, but you never will. So grab this book, grab your notes, make an appointment with your daughter, and have the kind of heart-to-heart talks that both of you deserve.

Talk to Your Daughter About God's Plan for Her Life

"For I know the plans I have for you"—[this is] the Lord's declaration—"plans for [your] welfare, not for disaster, to give you a future and a hope."

Jeremiah 29:11 HCSB

The Bible makes it clear: God has plans—very big plans—for you and your family. But He won't force His plans upon you—if you wish to experience the abundance that God has in store, you must be willing to accept His will and follow His Son.

As Christians, you and your family members should ask yourselves this question: "How closely can we make our plans match God's plans?" The more closely you manage to follow the path that God intends for your lives, the better.

Your daughter undoubtedly has concerns about her present circumstances, and you should encourage her to take those concerns to God in prayer. Your daughter has hopes and dreams. You should encourage her to talk to God about those dreams. And your daughter is making plans for the future, a future by the way, that only the Creator can see. You should ask her to let God guide her steps.

So remember that God intends to use you—and your daughter—in wonderful, unexpected ways. And it's up to you to seek His plan for your own life while encouraging your daughter to do the same. When you do, you'll discover that God's plans are grand and glorious . . . more glorious than either of you can imagine.

More from God's Word About
God's Guidance

The Lord says, "I will make you wise and show you where to go. I will guide you and watch over you."

Psalm 32:8 NCV

The true children of God are those who let God's Spirit lead them.

Romans 8:14 NCV

Lord, You light my lamp; my God illuminates my darkness.

Psalm 18:28 HCSB

In all your ways acknowledge Him, and He shall direct your paths.

Proverbs 3:6 NKJV

Every morning he wakes me. He teaches me to listen like a student. The Lord God helps me learn . . . .

Isaiah 50:4-5 NCV

We know that all things work together for the good of those who love God: those who are called according to His purpose.

Romans 8:28 HCSB

But as it is written: What no eye has seen and no ear has heard, and what has never come into a man's heart, is what God has prepared for those who love Him.

1 Corinthians 2:9 HCSB

In Him we were also made His inheritance, predestined according to the purpose of the One who works out everything in agreement with the decision of His will.

Ephesians 1:11 HCSB

Yet Lord, You are our Father; we are the clay, and You are our potter; we all are the work of Your hands.

Isaiah 64:8 HCSB

He replied, "Every plant that My Heavenly Father didn't plant will be uprooted."

Matthew 15:13 HCSB

More Food for Thought About God's Guidance

With God, it's never "Plan B" or "second best." It's always "Plan A." And, if we let Him, He'll make something beautiful of our lives.

Gloria Gaither

God has a plan for the life of every Christian. Every circumstance, every turn of destiny, all things work together for your good and for His glory.

Billy Graham

God wants us to serve Him with a willing spirit, one that would choose no other way.

Beth Moore

God will never lead you where His strength cannot keep you.

Barbara Johnson

God has a course mapped out for your life, and all the inadequacies in the world will not change His mind. He will be with you every step of the way. And though it may take time, He has a celebration planned for when you cross over the "Red Seas" of your life.

Charles Swindoll

The Lord never makes a mistake. One day, when we are in heaven, I'm sure we shall see the answers to all the whys. My, how often I have asked, "Why?" In heaven, we shall see God's side of the embroidery.

Corrie ten Boom

If you believe in a God who controls the big things, you have to believe in a God who controls the little things. It is we, of course, to whom things look "little" or "big."

Elisabeth Elliot

Ours is an intentional God, brimming over with motive and mission. He never does things capriciously or decides with the flip of a coin.

Joni Eareckson Tada

GATHER YOUR THOUGHTS
Write Down at Least Three Things That Your Daughter Needs to Hear from You About God's Guidance

_____

_____

_____

_____

_____

_____

_____

_____

_____

_____

_____

_____

Remind Your Daughter That Faith Can Move Mountains

I assure you: If anyone says to this mountain, "Be lifted up and thrown into the sea," and does not doubt in his heart, but believes that what he says will happen, it will be done for him.

Mark 11:23 HCSB

Because we live in a demanding world, all of us, parents and children alike, have mountains to climb and mountains to move. Moving those mountains requires faith. And the experience of trying, with God's help, to move mountains builds character.

Faith, like a tender seedling, can be nurtured or neglected. When we nurture our faith through prayer, meditation, and worship, God blesses our lives and lifts our spirits. But when we fail to consult the Father early and often, we do ourselves and our loved ones a profound disservice.

Are you a mountain-moving person whose faith is evident for your daughter to see? Or, are you a spiritual shrinking violet? As you think about the answer to that question, consider this: God needs more people—and especially more parents—who are willing to move mountains for His glory and for His kingdom.

Every life—including your daughter's life—is a series of wins and losses. Every step of the way, through every triumph and every trial, God walks with your child, ready and willing to strengthen her. So the next time your daughter's character is being tested, remind her to take her concerns to God. And while you're at it, remind her that no problem is too big for Creator of the universe.

With God, all things are possible, and He stands ready to open a world of possibilities to your daughter and to you . . . if you have faith.

More from God's Word About Worship

I rejoiced with those who said to me, "Let us go to the house of the Lord."

Psalm 122:1 HCSB

And every day they devoted themselves to meeting together in the temple complex, and broke bread from house to house. They ate their food with gladness and simplicity of heart, praising God and having favor with all the people. And every day the Lord added those being saved to them.

Acts 2:46-47 HCSB

For we walk by faith, not by sight.

2 Corinthians 5:7 HCSB

But an hour is coming, and is now here, when the true worshipers will worship the Father in spirit and truth. Yes, the Father wants such people to worship Him. God is Spirit, and those who worship Him must worship in spirit and truth.

John 4:23-24 HCSB

So that at the name of Jesus every knee should bow—of those who are in heaven and on earth and under the earth—and every tongue should confess that Jesus Christ is Lord, to the glory of God the Father.

Philippians 2:10-11 HCSB

If you do not stand firm in your faith, then you will not stand at all.

Isaiah 7:9 HCSB

Be alert, stand firm in the faith, be brave and strong.

1 Corinthians 16:13 HCSB

Now faith is the reality of what is hoped for, the proof of what is not seen.

Hebrews 11:1 HCSB

Now without faith it is impossible to please God, for the one who draws near to Him must believe that He exists and rewards those who seek Him.

Hebrews 11:6 HCSB

More Food for Thought About
Faith and Worship

Faith is seeing light with the eyes of your heart, when the eyes of your body see only darkness.

Barbara Johnson

Grace calls you to get up, throw off your blanket of helplessness, and to move on through life in faith.

Kay Arthur

Just as our faith strengthens our prayer life, so do our prayers deepen our faith. Let us pray often, starting today, for a deeper, more powerful faith.

Shirley Dobson

Faith does not concern itself with the entire journey. One step is enough.

Mrs. Charles E. Cowman

If God chooses to remain silent, faith is content.

Ruth Bell Graham

When you and I place our faith in Jesus Christ and invite Him to come live within us, the Holy Spirit comes upon us, and the power of God overshadows us, and the life of Jesus is born within us.

Anne Graham Lotz

Sometimes the very essence of faith is trusting God in the midst of things He knows good and well we cannot comprehend.

Beth Moore

Faith is trusting in advance what will only make sense in reverse.

Philip Yancey

Faith is nothing more or less than actively trusting God.

Catherine Marshall

GATHER YOUR THOUGHTS
Write Down at Least Three Things That Your Daughter Needs to Hear from You About Faith and Worship

_____

_____

_____

_____

_____

_____

_____

_____

_____

_____

_____

_____

_____

_____

Remind Your Daughter That Hard Work Pays Big Dividends

We must do the works of Him who sent Me while it is day. Night is coming when no one can work.

John 9:4 HCSB

Has your daughter acquired the habit of doing first things first, or is she one of those teens who puts off important work until the last minute? The answer to this simple question will help determine how well she does in school, how quickly she succeeds in the workplace, and how much satisfaction she derives along the way.

God's Word teaches the value of hard work. In his second letter to the Thessalonians, Paul warns, "if any would not work, neither should he eat" (3:10 KJV). And the Book of Proverbs proclaims, "One who is slack in his work is brother to one who destroys" (18:9 NIV). In short, God has created a world in which diligence is rewarded and laziness is not. And as a parent, it's up to you to convey this message to your daughter using both words and examples (with a decided emphasis on the latter).

Your daughter will undoubtedly have countless opportunities to accomplish great things—but she should not expect life's greatest rewards to be delivered on a silver platter. Instead, she should pray as if everything depended upon God, but work as if everything depended upon herself. When she does, she can expect very big payoffs indeed.

More from God's Word About Success

Success, success to you, and success to those who help you, for your God will help you . . . .

1 Chronicles 12:18 NIV

But as for you, be strong and do not give up, for your work will be rewarded.

2 Chronicles 15:7 NIV

Let us not become weary in doing good, for at the proper time we will reap a harvest if we do not give up.

Galatians 6:9 NIV

You need to persevere so that when you have done the will of God, you will receive what he has promised.

Hebrews 10:36 NIV

The one who understands a matter finds success, and the one who trusts in the Lord will be happy.

Proverbs 16:20 HCSB

Whatever you do, do it enthusiastically, as something done for the Lord and not for men.

Colossians 3:23 HCSB

Whatever your hands find to do, do with [all] your strength.

Ecclesiastes 9:10 HCSB

He did it with all his heart. So he prospered.

2 Chronicles 31:21 NKJV

Don't work only while being watched, in order to please men, but as slaves of Christ, do God's will from your heart. Render service with a good attitude, as to the Lord and not to men.

Ephesians 6:6-7 HCSB

Lazy hands make a man poor, but diligent hands bring wealth.

Proverbs 10:4 NIV

More Food for Thought About Success

Ordinary work, which is what most of us do most of the time, is ordained by God every bit as much as is the extraordinary.

Elisabeth Elliot

You can't climb the ladder of life with your hands in your pockets.

Barbara Johnson

Great relief and satisfaction can come from seeking God's priorities for us in each season, discerning what is "best" in the midst of many noble opportunities, and pouring our most excellent energies into those things.

Beth Moore

In the very place where God has put us, whatever its limitations, whatever kind of work it may be, we may indeed serve the Lord Christ.

Elisabeth Elliot

If you honor God with your work, He will honor you because of your work.

Marie T. Freeman

Few things fire up a person's commitment like dedication to excellence.

John Maxwell

Thank God every morning when you get up that you have something which must be done, whether you like it or not. Work breeds a hundred virtues that idleness never knows.

Charles Kingsley

It may be that the day of judgment will dawn tomorrow; in that case, we shall gladly stop working for a better tomorrow. But not before.

Dietrich Bonhoeffer

God provides the ingredients for our daily bread but expects us to do the baking. With our own hands!

Barbara Johnson

GATHER YOUR THOUGHTS
Write Down at Least Three Things That Your Daughter Needs to Hear from You About Success

Talk About the Need to Manage Time Wisely

So teach us to number our days,
that we may gain a heart of wisdom.

Psalm 90:12 NKJV

Time is a nonrenewable gift from God. But sometimes, all of us—both parents and children alike—treat our time here on earth as if it were not a gift at all: We may be tempted to invest our lives in trivial pursuits and petty diversions. Instead of doing what needs to be done now, we procrastinate. Yet our Father beckons each of us to a higher calling.

If you intend to be a responsible parent, you must teach your daughter to use time responsibly. After all, each waking moment holds the potential to do a good deed, to say a kind word, to fulfill a personal responsibility, or to offer a heartfelt prayer.

Time is a perishable commodity: we must use it or lose it. So your child's challenge (and yours) is to use the gift of time wisely. To do any less is an affront to the Creator and a prescription for disappointment.

More from God's Word About Time Management

Therefore, get your minds ready for action, being self-disciplined, and set your hope completely on the grace to be brought to you at the revelation of Jesus Christ.

1 Peter 1:13 HCSB

When you make a vow to God, don't delay fulfilling it, because He does not delight in fools. Fulfill what you vow.

Ecclesiastes 5:4 HCSB

If you do nothing in a difficult time, your strength is limited.

Proverbs 24:10 HCSB

Working together with Him, we also appeal to you: "Don't receive God's grace in vain." For He says: In an acceptable time, I heard you, and in the day of salvation, I helped you. Look, now is the acceptable time; look, now is the day of salvation.

2 Corinthians 6:1-2 HCSB

Be strong and courageous, and do the work. Don't be afraid or discouraged, for the Lord God, my God, is with you. He won't leave you or forsake you.

1 Chronicles 28:20 HCSB

More Food for Thought About
Time Management

God has a present will for your life. It is neither chaotic nor utterly exhausting. In the midst of many good choices vying for your time, He will give you the discernment to recognize what is best.

Beth Moore

Our leisure, even our play, is a matter of serious concern. There is no neutral ground in the universe: every square inch, every split second, is claimed by God and counterclaimed by Satan.

C. S. Lewis

There were endless demands on Jesus' time. Still he was able to make that amazing claim of "completing the work you gave me to do." (John 17:4 NIV)

Elisabeth Elliot

Stay busy. Get proper exercise. Eat the right foods. Don't spend time watching TV, lying in bed, or napping all day.

Truett Cathy

The work of God is appointed. There is always enough time to do the will of God.

Elisabeth Elliot

Our time is short! The time we can invest for God, in creative things, in receiving our fellowmen for Christ, is short!

Billy Graham

Time here on earth is limited . . . use it or lose it!

Anonymous

Frustration is not the will of God. There is time to do anything and everything that God wants us to do.

Elisabeth Elliot

GATHER YOUR THOUGHTS
Write Down at Least Three Things That
Your Daughter Needs to Hear
from You About Time Management

_____

_____

_____

_____

_____

_____

_____

_____

_____

_____

_____

_____

_____

_____

Tell Your Daughter That It's Better to Be Right Than Popular

But run away from the evil young people like to do.
Try hard to live right and to have faith, love, and peace,
together with those who trust in the Lord from pure hearts.

2 Timothy 2:22 NCV

I f your daughter is like most young women, she will seek the admiration of her friends and classmates. But the eagerness to please others should never overshadow her eagerness to please God. God has big plans for your daughter, and if your child intends to fulfill God's plans by following God's Son, then your daughter must seek to please the Father first and always.

Everyday life is an adventure in decision-making. Each day, your daughter will make countless decisions that will hopefully bring her closer to God. When she obeys God's commandments, she inevitably experiences God's abundance and His peace. But, if your child turns her back on God by disobeying Him, she will unintentionally invite Old Man Trouble to stop by for an extended visit.

Do you want your daughter to be successful and happy? Then encourage her to study God's Word and live by it. If your daughter follows that advice, then when she faces a difficult choice or a powerful temptation (as she most certainly will), she'll be prepared to meet the enemy head-on.

So, as a thoughtful parent, your task is straightforward: encourage your child to seek God's approval in every aspect of her life. Does this sound too simple? Perhaps it is simple, but it is also the only way for your daughter to reap the marvelous riches that God has in store for her.

More from God's Word About
Obedience to God

Make the most of every opportunity.

Colossians 4:5 NIV

Let us not lose heart in doing good, for in due time we shall reap if we do not grow weary. So then, while we have opportunity, let us do good to all men, and especially to those who are of the household of the faith.

Galatians 6:9-10 NASB

Dear brothers and sisters, whenever trouble comes your way, let it be an opportunity for joy. For when your faith is tested, your endurance has a chance to grow. So let it grow, for when your endurance is fully developed, you will be strong in character and ready for anything.

James 1:2-4 NLT

Remember ye not the former things, neither consider the things of old. Behold, I will do a new thing . . . .

Isaiah 43:18-19 KJV

For the eyes of the Lord are over the righteous, and his ears are open unto their prayers: but the face of the Lord is against them that do evil.

1 Peter 3:12 KJV

Blessed are the pure of heart, for they will see God.

Matthew 5:8 NIV

But seek first his kingdom and his righteousness, and all these things will be given to you as well.

Matthew 6:33 NIV

The Lord will not reject his people; he will not abandon his own special possession. Judgement will come again for the righteous, and those who are upright will have a reward.

Psalm 94:14-15 NLT

The righteous shall flourish like the palm tree: he shall grow like a cedar in Lebanon.

Psalm 92:12 KJV

More Food for Thought About Obedience to God

Our afflictions are designed not to break us but to bend us toward the eternal and the holy.

Barbara Johnson

Becoming pure is a process of spiritual growth, and taking seriously the confession of sin during prayer time moves that process along, causing us to purge our life of practices that displease God.

Elizabeth George

Holiness has never been the driving force of the majority. It is, however, mandatory for anyone who wants to enter the kingdom.

Elisabeth Elliot

He doesn't need an abundance of words. He doesn't need a dissertation about your life. He just wants your attention. He wants your heart.

Kathy Troccoli

The great thing is to be found at one's post as a child of God, living each day as though it were our last, but planning as though our world might last a hundred years.

C. S. Lewis

We have a decision to make—to turn away from sin or to be miserable and suffer the consequences of continual disobedience.

Vonette Bright

Learning God's truth and getting it into our heads is one thing, but living God's truth and getting it into our characters is quite something else.

Warren Wiersbe

I believe the reason so many are failing today is that they have not disciplined themselves to read God's Word consistently, day in and day out, and to apply it to every situation in life.

Kay Arthur

GATHER YOUR THOUGHTS
Write Down at Least Three Things That Your Daughter Needs to Hear from You About Obedience to God

Tell Your Daughter That Optimism Pays and Pessimism Doesn't

But if we look forward to something we don't have yet, we must wait patiently and confidently.

Romans 8:25 NLT

A re you an optimistic, hopeful, enthusiastic Christian? You should be. After all, as a believer, you have every reason to be optimistic about life here on earth and life eternal. As English clergyman William Ralph Inge observed, "No Christian should be a pessimist, for Christianity is a system of radical optimism." Inge's words are most certainly true, but sometimes, you and your loved ones may find yourselves pulled down by the inevitable demands and worries of life here on earth. If so, it's time to ask yourself this question: what's bothering you, and why?

If you're worried by the inevitable challenges of everyday living, God wants to have a little talk with you. After all, the ultimate battle has already been won on the cross at Calvary. And if your life has been transformed by Christ's sacrifice, then you, as a recipient of God's grace, have every reason to live courageously.

Are you willing to trust God's plans for your life, and will you encourage your daughter to do the same? Hopefully so because even when the challenges of the day seem daunting, God remains steadfast. And, so should you.

So make this promise to yourself and keep it—vow to be a hope-filled parent. Think optimistically about your life, your profession, your family, your future, and your purpose for living. Trust your hopes, not your fears. Take time to celebrate God's glorious creation. And then, when you've filled your heart with hope and gladness, share your optimism with every member of your family. They'll be better for it, and so will you.

More from God's Word About Optimism

Make me hear joy and gladness.

Psalm 51:8 NKJV

For God has not given us a spirit of fearfulness, but one of power, love, and sound judgment.

2 Timothy 1:7 HCSB

My cup runs over. Surely goodness and mercy shall follow me all the days of my life; and I will dwell in the house of the Lord Forever.

Psalm 23:5-6 NKJV

I am able to do all things through Him who strengthens me.

Philippians 4:13 HCSB

Lord, I turn my hope to You. My God, I trust in You.

Psalm 25:1-2 HCSB

More Food for Thought About Optimism

It is a remarkable thing that some of the most optimistic and enthusiastic people you will meet are those who have been through intense suffering.

Warren Wiersbe

The Christian lifestyle is not one of legalistic do's and don'ts, but one that is positive, attractive, and joyful.

Vonette Bright

The popular idea of faith is of a certain obstinate optimism: the hope, tenaciously held in the face of trouble, that the universe is fundamentally friendly and things may get better.

J. I. Packer

The essence of optimism is that it takes no account of the present, but it is a source of inspiration, of vitality, and of hope. Where others have resigned, it enables a man to hold his head high, to claim the future for himself, and not abandon it to his enemy.

Dietrich Bonhoeffer

The people whom I have seen succeed best in life have always been cheerful and hopeful people who went about their business with a smile on their faces.

Charles Kingsley

Developing a positive attitude means working continually to find what is uplifting and encouraging.

Barbara Johnson

Keep your feet on the ground, but let your heart soar as high as it will. Refuse to be average or to surrender to the chill of your spiritual environment.

A. W. Tozer

If our hearts have been attuned to God through an abiding faith in Christ, the result will be joyous optimism and good cheer.

Billy Graham

Christ can put a spring in your step and a thrill in your heart. Optimism and cheerfulness are products of knowing Christ.

Billy Graham

GATHER YOUR THOUGHTS
Write Down at Least Three Things That Your Daughter Needs to Hear from You About Optimism

Talk to Your Daughter About the Power of Prayer

So I say to you, keep asking, and it will be given to you.
Keep searching, and you will find.
Keep knocking, and the door will be opened to you.

Luke 11:9 HCSB

Genuine, heartfelt prayer produces powerful changes in us and in our world. When we lift our hearts to God, we open ourselves to a never-ending source of divine wisdom and infinite love. So as a Christian parent, you must make certain that your child understands the power of prayer and the need for prayer. And the best way to do so, of course, is by example.

Is prayer an integral part of your family's life, or is it a hit-or-miss habit? Do you "pray without ceasing," or is your prayer life an afterthought? Do you regularly honor God in the solitude of the early morning darkness, or do you bow your head only when others are watching?

The quality of your daughter's spiritual life will be in direct proportion to the quality of her prayer life. Prayer changes things, and it will change her. So when you can tell she's turning things over in her mind, encourage her to turn them over to God in prayer. And while you're at it, don't limit your family's prayers to meals or to bedtime. Make sure that your family is constantly praying about things great and small because God is listening, and He wants to hear from you now.

More from God's Word About Prayer

The intense prayer of the righteous is very powerful.

James 5:16 HCSB

Let the words of my mouth and the meditation of my heart be acceptable in Your sight, O Lord, my strength and my Redeemer.

Psalm 19:14 NKJV

Yet He often withdrew to deserted places and prayed.

Luke 5:16 HCSB

Don't worry about anything, but in everything, through prayer and petition with thanksgiving, let your requests be made known to God.

Philippians 4:6 HCSB

Rejoice in hope; be patient in affliction; be persistent in prayer.

Romans 12:12 HCSB

You do not have, because you do not ask God.

James 4:2 NIV

Verily, verily, I say unto you, He that believeth on me, the works that I do shall he do also; and greater works than these shall he do; because I go unto my Father. And whatsoever ye shall ask in my name, that will I do, that the Father may be glorified in the Son. If ye shall ask any thing in my name, I will do it.

John 14:12-14 KJV

You did not choose me, but I chose you and appointed you to go and bear fruit—fruit that will last. Then the Father will give you whatever you ask in my name.

John 15:16 NIV

Let us hold fast the confession of our hope without wavering, for He who promised is faithful.

Hebrews 10:23 NASB

More Food for Thought About Prayer

By asking in Jesus' name, we're making a request not only in His authority, but also for His interests and His benefit.

Shirley Dobson

When will we realize that we're not troubling God with our questions and concerns? His heart is open to hear us— his touch nearer than our next thought—as if no one in the world existed but us. Our very personal God wants to hear from us personally.

Gigi Graham Tchividjian

God uses our most stumbling, faltering faith-steps as the open door to His doing for us "more than we ask or think."

Catherine Marshall

Often I have made a request of God with earnest pleadings even backed up with Scripture, only to have Him say "No" because He had something better in store.

Ruth Bell Graham

God makes prayer as easy as possible for us. He's completely approachable and available, and He'll never mock or upbraid us for bringing our needs before Him.

Shirley Dobson

When you ask God to do something, don't ask timidly; put your whole heart into it.

Marie T. Freeman

When trials come your way—as inevitably they will—do not run away. Run to your God and Father.

Kay Arthur

All we have to do is to acknowledge our need, move from self-sufficiency to dependence, and ask God to become our hiding place.

Bill Hybels

God will help us become the people we are meant to be, if only we will ask Him.

Hannah Whitall Smith

GATHER YOUR THOUGHTS
Write Down at Least Three Things That Your Daughter Needs to Hear from You About Prayer

Remind Your Daughter to Celebrate the Gift of Life

This is the day the Lord has made;
let us rejoice and be glad in it.
Psalm 118:24 HCSB

The 118th Psalm reminds us that today, like every other day, is a cause for celebration. God gives us this day; He fills it to the brim with possibilities, and He challenges us to use it for His purposes. The day is presented to us fresh and clean at midnight, free of charge, but we must beware: Today is a non-renewable resource—once it's gone, it's gone forever. Our responsibility, of course, is to use this day in the service of God's will and according to His commandments.

If your daughter is like most people, she may, at times, fall victim to the negativity and cynicism of our negative age. And if that happens, it's up to you to remind her that every day is a gift and that she should treasure the time that God has given her.

The Christian life should be a triumphal celebration, a daily exercise in thanksgiving and praise. Encourage your daughter to join that celebration. And while you're at it, make sure that you've joined in the celebration, too.

More from God's Word About Cheerfulness

Be cheerful. Keep things in good repair. Keep your spirits up. Think in harmony. Be agreeable. Do all that, and the God of love and peace will be with you for sure.

2 Corinthians 13:11 MSG

Jacob said, "For what a relief it is to see your friendly smile. It is like seeing the smile of God!"

Genesis 33:10 NLT

Do everything readily and cheerfully—no bickering, no second-guessing allowed! Go out into the world uncorrupted, a breath of fresh air in this squalid and polluted society. Provide people with a glimpse of good living and of the living God. Carry the light-giving Message into the night.

Philippians 2:14-15 MSG

Is anyone happy? Let him sing songs of praise . . .

James 5:13 NIV

God loves a cheerful giver.

2 Corinthians 9:7 NIV

Celebrate God all day, every day. I mean, revel in him!

Philippians 4:4 MSG

David and the whole house of Israel were celebrating before the Lord.

2 Samuel 6:5 HCSB

Their sorrow was turned into rejoicing and their mourning into a holiday. They were to be days of feasting, rejoicing, and of sending gifts to one another and the poor.

Esther 9:22 HCSB

At the dedication of the wall of Jerusalem, they sent for the Levites wherever they lived and brought them to Jerusalem to celebrate the joyous dedication with thanksgiving and singing accompanied by cymbals, harps, and lyres.

Nehemiah 12:27 HCSB

These things I have spoken to you, that My joy may remain in you, and that your joy may be full.

John 15:11 NKJV

More Food for Thought About Cheerfulness

According to Jesus, it is God's will that His children be filled with the joy of life.

Catherine Marshall

If you can forgive the person you were, accept the person you are, and believe in the person you will become, you are headed for joy. So celebrate your life.

Barbara Johnson

Christ is the secret, the source, the substance, the center, and the circumference of all true and lasting gladness.

Mrs. Charles E. Cowman

When the dream of our heart is one that God has planted there, a strange happiness flows into us. At that moment, all of the spiritual resources of the universe are released to help us. Our praying is then at one with the will of God and becomes a channel for the Creator's purposes for us and our world.

Catherine Marshall

Joy is a by-product not of happy circumstances, education or talent, but of a healthy relationship with God and a determination to love Him no matter what.

Barbara Johnson

God knows everything. He can manage everything, and He loves us. Surely this is enough for a fullness of joy that is beyond words.

Hannah Whitall Smith

What is your focus today? Joy comes when it is Jesus first, others second . . . then you.

Kay Arthur

Joy is the serious business of heaven.

C. S. Lewis

Give yourself a gift today: be present with yourself. God is. Enjoy your own personality. God does.

Barbara Johnson

GATHER YOUR THOUGHTS
Write Down at Least Three Things That Your Daughter Needs to Hear from You About Cheerfulness

Remind Your Daughter That Character *Really* Counts

People with integrity have firm footing,
but those who follow crooked paths will slip and fall.

Proverbs 10:9 NLT

It has been said that character is what we are when nobody is watching. How true. When we do things that we know aren't right, we try to hide them from our families and friends. But even if we successfully conceal our sins from the world, we can never conceal our sins from God.

Charles Swindoll correctly observed, "Nothing speaks louder or more powerfully than a life of integrity." Wise parents agree.

Integrity is built slowly over a lifetime. It is the sum of every right decision and every honest word. It is forged on the anvil of honorable work and polished by the twin virtues of honesty and fairness. Integrity is a precious thing—difficult to build but easy to tear down.

Living a life of integrity isn't always the easiest way, especially for a young person like your daughter. After all, she inhabits a world that presents her with countless temptations to stray far from God's path. So as a parent, your job is to remind her (again and again) that whenever she's confronted with sin, she should walk—or better yet run—in the opposite direction. And the good news is this: When your daughter makes up her mind to walk with Jesus every day, her character will take care of itself . . . and she won't need to look over her shoulder to see who, besides God, is watching.

More from God's Word About
Truth

Be diligent to present yourself approved to God, a worker who doesn't need to be ashamed, correctly teaching the word of truth.

2 Timothy 2:15 HCSB

I have no greater joy than this: to hear that my children are walking in the truth.

3 John 1:4 HCSB

When the Spirit of truth comes, He will guide you into all the truth.

John 16:13 HCSB

You will know the truth, and the truth will set you free.

John 8:32 HCSB

As the water reflects the face, so the heart reflects the person.

Proverbs 27:19 HCSB

We also rejoice in our afflictions, because we know that affliction produces endurance, endurance produces proven character, and proven character produces hope.

Romans 5:3-4 HCSB

A good name is to be chosen rather than great riches, loving favor rather than silver and gold.

Proverbs 22:1 NKJV

Do not be deceived: "Evil company corrupts good habits."

1 Corinthians 15:33 NKJV

For everyone who practices wicked things hates the light and avoids it, so that his deeds may not be exposed. But anyone who lives by the truth comes to the light, so that his works may be shown to be accomplished by God.

John 3:20–21 HCSB

In all things showing yourself to be a pattern of good works; in doctrine showing integrity, reverence, incorruptibility . . . .

Titus 2:7 NKJV

More Food for Thought About Truth

There is something about having endured great loss that brings purity of purpose and strength of character.

Barbara Johnson

Often, our character is at greater risk in prosperity than in adversity.

Beth Moore

We actually are, at present, creatures whose character must be, in some respects, a horror to God, as it is, when we really see it, a horror to ourselves. This I believe to be a fact: and I notice that the holier a man is, the more fully he is aware of that fact.

C. S. Lewis

Integrity is the glue that holds our way of life together. We must constantly strive to keep our integrity intact. When wealth is lost, nothing is lost; when health is lost, something is lost; when character is lost, all is lost.

Billy Graham

Each one of us is God's special work of art. Through us, He teaches and inspires, delights and encourages, informs and uplifts all those who view our lives. God, the master artist, is most concerned about expressing Himself—His thoughts and His intentions—through what He paints in our characters.

Joni Eareckson Tada

Integrity is not a given factor in everyone's life. It is a result of self-discipline, inner trust, and a decision to be relentlessly honest in all situations in our lives.

John Maxwell

Honesty has a beautiful and refreshing simplicity about it. No ulterior motives. No hidden meanings. As honesty and integrity characterize our lives, there will be no need to manipulate others.

Charles Swindoll

The single most important element in any human relationship is honesty—with oneself, with God, and with others.

Catherine Marshall

Sow an act, and you reap a habit. Sow a habit and you reap a character. Sow a character and you reap a destiny.

Anonymous

GATHER YOUR THOUGHTS
Write Down at Least Three Things That Your Daughter Needs to Hear from You About Truth

_____

_____

_____

_____

_____

_____

_____

_____

_____

_____

_____

_____

Remind Your Daughter That She Still Has Lots to Learn

*Apply yourself to instruction
and listen to words of knowledge.*

Proverbs 23:12 HCSB

As long as we live, we should continue to learn, and we should encourage our children to do likewise. But sometimes the job of teaching our kids seems to be a thankless one. Why? Because sometimes our children pay scant attention to the educational opportunities that we adults work so hard to provide for them.

Education is the tool by which all of us—parents and children alike—come to know and appreciate the world in which we live. It is the shining light that snuffs out the darkness of ignorance and poverty. Education is freedom just as surely as ignorance is a form of bondage. Education is not a luxury; it is a necessity and a powerful tool for good in this world.

When it comes to learning life's most important lessons, we can either do things the easy way or the hard way. The easy way can be summed up as follows: when God teaches us a lesson, we learn it . . . the first time. Unfortunately, too many of us learn much more slowly than that.

When we resist God's instruction, He continues to teach, whether we like it or not. Our challenge, then, is to discern God's lessons from the experiences of everyday life. Hopefully, we learn those lessons sooner rather than later because the sooner we do, the sooner He can move on to the next lesson and the next and the next.

So your challenge, as a thoughtful parent, is straightforward: to convince your daughter that she still has much to learn, even if she would prefer to believe otherwise.

More from God's Word About Wisdom and Maturity

A wise heart accepts commands, but foolish lips will be destroyed.

Proverbs 10:8 HCSB

The fear of the Lord is the beginning of knowledge, but fools despise wisdom and discipline.

Proverbs 1:7 NIV

The knowledge of the secrets of the kingdom of heaven has been given to you . . . .

Matthew 13:11 NIV

It is not good to have zeal without knowledge, nor to be hasty and miss the way.

Proverbs 19:2 NIV

But grow in grace, and in the knowledge of our Lord and Saviour Jesus Christ . . . .

2 Peter 3:18 KJV

Continue in what you have learned and have become convinced of, because you know those from whom you learned it, and how from infancy you have known the holy Scriptures, which are able to make you wise for salvation through faith in Christ Jesus.

2 Timothy 3:14-15 NIV

Consider it pure joy, my brothers, whenever you face trials of many kinds, because you know that the testing of your faith develops perseverance. Perseverance must finish its work so that you may be mature and complete, not lacking anything.

James 1:2-4 NIV

You must follow the Lord your God and fear Him. You must keep His commands and listen to His voice; you must worship Him and remain faithful to Him.

Deuteronomy 13:4 HCSB

More Food for Thought About Maturity

The wonderful thing about God's schoolroom is that we get to grade our own papers. You see, He doesn't test us so He can learn how well we're doing. He tests us so we can discover how well we're doing.

Charles Swindoll

True learning can take place at every age of life, and it doesn't have to be in the curriculum plan.

Suzanne Dale Ezell

While chastening is always difficult, if we look to God for the lesson we should learn, we will see spiritual fruit.

Vonette Bright

The wise man gives proper appreciation in his life to his past. He learns to sift the sawdust of heritage in order to find the nuggets that make the current moment have any meaning.

Grady Nutt

It's the things you learn after you know it all that really count.

Vance Havner

Our loving God uses difficulty in our lives to burn away the sin of self and build faith and spiritual power.

Bill Bright

I don't doubt that the Holy Spirit guides your decisions from within when you make them with the intention of pleasing God. The error would be to think that He speaks only within, whereas in reality He speaks also through Scripture, the Church, Christian friends, and books.

C. S. Lewis

God is able to take mistakes, when they are committed to Him, and make of them something for our good and for His glory.

Ruth Bell Graham

GATHER YOUR THOUGHTS
Write Down at Least Three Things That
Your Daughter Needs to Hear
from You About Maturity

_____

_____

_____

_____

_____

_____

_____

_____

_____

_____

_____

_____

_____

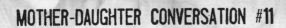

Remind Your Daughter That It's Dangerous Out There, So She Should Slow Down, Buckle Up, and Avoid Impulsive Behaviors

The sensible see danger and take cover;
the foolish keep going and are punished.

Proverbs 27:12 HCSB

It's a nightmare that, from time to time, crosses the mind of every loving parent: the thought that serious injury might befall a child. These parental fears are reinforced by tragic accidents that, all too often, are splashed across the headlines of our local news.

Since no one can deny that far too many young people behave recklessly, it's your job, as a responsible parent, to do everything within your power to ensure that your child is far more safety conscious than the norm. In short, you should become your family's safety advisor. You should be vocal, you should be persistent, you should be consistent, and you should be informed.

Maturity and safety go hand in hand. So, as your daughter becomes a more mature young woman, she'll naturally, if gradually, acquire the habit of looking before she leaps. And that's good because when young people leap first and look second, they often engage in destructive behavior that they soon come to regret.

So don't hesitate to talk to your daughter about safety, don't hesitate to teach her safe behavior, don't hesitate to plan for her safety, and, when necessary, don't hesitate to limit her access to people and places that might cause her physical, emotional, or spiritual harm.

Being a strict, safety-conscious parent may not be the quickest path to parental popularity. But it's one of the best things you can do to help your daughter enjoy a long, happy, productive life.

More from God's Word About
Safety and Sensibility

Grow a wise heart—you'll do yourself a favor; keep a clear head—you'll find a good life.

Proverbs 19:8 MSG

Follow my advice, my son; always treasure my commands. Obey them and live! Guard my teachings as your most precious possession. Tie them on your fingers as a reminder. Write them deep within your heart.

Proverbs 7:1-3 NLT

Enthusiasm without knowledge is not good. If you act too quickly, you might make a mistake.

Proverbs 19:2 NCV

For God has not given us a spirit of fearfulness, but one of power, love, and sound judgment.

2 Timothy 1:7 HCSB

Therefore, everyone who hears these words of Mine and acts on them will be like a sensible man who built his house on the rock. The rain fell, the rivers rose, and the winds blew and pounded that house. Yet it didn't collapse, because its foundation was on the rock.

Matthew 7:24-25 HCSB

More Food for Thought About Safety

Knowledge is horizontal. Wisdom is vertical; it comes down from above.

Billy Graham

God's plan for our guidance is for us to grow gradually in wisdom before we get to the cross roads.

Bill Hybels

The more wisdom enters our hearts, the more we will be able to trust our hearts in difficult situations.

John Eldredge

Patience is the companion of wisdom.

St. Augustine

Wise people listen to wise instruction, especially instruction from the Word of God.

Warren Wiersbe

If you lack knowledge, go to school. If you lack wisdom, get on your knees.

Vance Havner

The fruit of wisdom is Christlikeness, peace, humility, and love. And, the root of it is faith in Christ as the manifested wisdom of God.

J. I. Packer

Wisdom is knowledge applied. Head knowledge is useless on the battlefield. Knowledge stamped on the heart makes one wise.

Beth Moore

The person who is wise spiritually, who is a true Christian, builds his life and performs his duties carefully, realizing the great substance and importance involved.

John MacArthur

GATHER YOUR THOUGHTS
Write Down at Least Three Things That
Your Daughter Needs to Hear
from You About Safety

_____

_____

_____

_____

_____

_____

_____

_____

_____

_____

_____

_____

_____

Talk to Your Daughter About the Trap of Materialism

No one can serve two masters.
The person will hate one master and love the other,
or will follow one master and refuse to follow the other.
You cannot serve both God and worldly riches.

Matthew 6:24 NCV

Your daughter inhabits a world in which material possessions are, at times, glamorized and, at other times, almost worshipped. The media often glorifies material possessions above all else, but God most certainly does not. And it's up to you, as a responsible parent, to make certain that your child understands that materialism is a spiritual trap, a trap that should be avoided at all costs.

Martin Luther observed, "Many things I have tried to grasp and have lost. That which I have placed in God's hands I still have." His words apply to all of us. Our earthly riches are transitory; our spiritual riches, on the other hand, are everlasting.

If you find yourself wrapped up in the concerns of the material world, you can be sure that your family members are wrapped up in it, too. So how much stuff is too much stuff? It's a tough question for many of us, yet the answer is straightforward: When our possessions begin to interfere with our desire to know and serve God, then we own too many possessions, period.

On the grand stage of a well-lived life, material possessions should play a rather small role. Of course, we all need the basic necessities of life, but once we meet those needs for ourselves and for our families, the piling up of possessions creates more problems than it solves. Our real riches, of course, are not of this world. We are never really rich until we are rich in spirit.

So, if you or your family members find yourselves

wrapped up in the concerns of the material world, it's time to reorder your priorities. And, it's time to begin storing up riches that will endure throughout eternity—the spiritual kind.

More from God's Word About Worldliness

And He told them, "Watch out and be on guard against all greed, because one's life is not in the abundance of his possessions."

Luke 12:15 HCSB

For what does it benefit a man to gain the whole world yet lose his life? What can a man give in exchange for his life?

Mark 8:36-37 HCSB

Don't collect for yourselves treasures on earth, where moth and rust destroy and where thieves break in and steal. But collect for yourselves treasures in heaven, where neither moth nor rust destroys, and where thieves don't break in and steal. For where your treasure is, there your heart will be also.

Matthew 6:19-21 HCSB

Anyone trusting in his riches will fall, but the righteous will flourish like foliage.

Proverbs 11:28 HCSB

Let no one deceive himself. If anyone among you seems to be wise in this age, let him become a fool that he may become wise. For the wisdom of this world is foolishness with God. For it is written, "He catches the wise in their own craftiness."

1 Corinthians 3:18–19 NKJV

Do not love the world or the things in the world. If you love the world, the love of the Father is not in you.

1 John 2:15 NCV

For whatever is born of God overcomes the world. And this is the victory that has overcome the world—our faith.

1 John 5:4 NKJV

Religion that God our Father accepts as pure and faultless is this: to look after orphans and widows in their distress and to keep oneself from being polluted by the world.

James 1:27 NIV

If you lived on the world's terms, the world would love you as one of its own. But since I picked you to live on God's terms and no longer on the world's terms, the world is going to hate you.

John 15:19 MSG

More Food for Thought About Worldliness

The more we stuff ourselves with material pleasures, the less we seem to appreciate life.

Barbara Johnson

He who dies with the most toys . . . still dies.

Anonymous

The cross is laid on every Christian. It begins with the call to abandon the attachments of this world.

Dietrich Bonhoeffer

Greed is enslaving. The more you have, the more you want—until eventually avarice consumes you.

Kay Arthur

We own too many things that aren't worth owning.

Marie T. Freeman

As faithful stewards of what we have, ought we not to give earnest thought to our staggering surplus?

Elisabeth Elliot

Why is love of gold more potent than love of souls?

Lottie Moon

Getting a little greedy? Pray without seizing.

Anonymous

It's sobering to contemplate how much time, effort, sacrifice, compromise, and attention we give to acquiring and increasing our supply of something that is totally insignificant in eternity.

Anne Graham Lotz

GATHER YOUR THOUGHTS
Write Down at Least Three Things That
Your Daughter Needs to Hear
from You About Worldliness

_____

_____

_____

_____

_____

_____

_____

_____

_____

_____

_____

_____

_____

_____

Remind Your Daughter That She Must Always Treat Her Body with Respect

Do you not know that your body is a sanctuary of the Holy Spirit who is in you, whom you have from God? You are not your own, for you were bought at a price; therefore glorify God in your body.

1 Corinthians 6:19-20 HCSB

Your daughter inhabits a society that is filled to the brim with temptations, distractions, and distortions about sex. She is bombarded with images that glamorize sex outside marriage. In fact, she is subjected to daily pressures and problems that were largely unknown to earlier generations. At every corner, or so it seems, she is confronted with the message that premarital sex is a harmless activity, something that should be considered "recreational." But that message is a terrible lie with tragic consequences.

As a loving Christian parent, your job is to make sure that your daughter understands that sex before marriage isn't just wrong; it's also dangerous physically, dangerous emotionally, and dangerous spiritually.

Thankfully, the argument in favor of abstinence isn't a very hard case for parents to make, if they're willing to make it. Yet far too many parents are uncomfortable talking to their children about matters pertaining to sex. So they put off those important discussions, sometimes until it's too late. Please don't make that mistake. When the time is right, sit down with your child, have a frank conversation, and make the case for abstinence.

Abstinence is a part of God's plan for people who are not married. Period. But it doesn't stop there: abstinence is also the right thing to do, the smart thing to do, and the safe thing to do. Yet it isn't always the easy thing to do, and that's why strong parental support can be so helpful.

So, Mom, take time, lots of time, to talk with your daughter about the wisdom of waiting. It's her choice, a choice that will have a major impact upon her self-esteem, her self-image, her spiritual growth, and her future. Please do whatever you can to help her choose wisely.

More from God's Word About Treating Our Bodies with Respect

For this is God's will, your sanctification: that you abstain from sexual immorality, so that each of you knows how to possess his own vessel in sanctification and honor, not with lustful desires, like the Gentiles who don't know God.

1 Thessalonians 4:3-5 HCSB

Marriage must be respected by all, and the marriage bed kept undefiled, because God will judge immoral people and adulterers.

Hebrews 13:4 HCSB

Therefore do not let sin reign in your mortal body, so that you obey its desires.

Romans 6:12 HCSB

More Food for Thought About
Treating Our Bodies
with Respect

There may be no trumpet sound or loud applause when we make a right decision, just a calm sense of resolution and peace.

Gloria Gaither

The soul is the user, the body for use; hence the one is master, the other servant.

St. Ambrose

Although God causes all things to work together for good for His children, He still holds us accountable for our behavior.

Kay Arthur

God wants you to give Him your body. Some people do foolish things with their bodies. God wants your body as a holy sacrifice.

Warren Wiersbe

Our body is like armor, our soul like the warrior. Take care of both, and you will be ready for what comes.

Amma St. Syncletice

Discrepancies between values and practices create chaos in a person's life.

John Maxwell

Obedience is the outward expression of your love of God.

Henry Blackaby

Our body is a portable sanctuary through which we are daily experiencing the presence of God.

Richard Foster

A Christian should no more defile his body than a Jew would defile the temple.

Warren Wiersbe

GATHER YOUR THOUGHTS
Write Down at Least Three Things That
Your Daughter Needs to Hear
from You About Treating
Our Bodies with Respect

_____

_____

_____

_____

_____

_____

_____

_____

_____

_____

_____

Remind Your Daughter That She Will Reap What She Sows

Don't be deceived: God is not mocked. For whatever a man sows he will also reap, because the one who sows to his flesh will reap corruption from the flesh, but the one who sows to the Spirit will reap eternal life from the Spirit.

Galatians 6:7-8 HCSB

How hard is it for young people to act responsibly? Sometimes, when youngsters are beset by negative role models and unrelenting peer pressure, it can be very difficult for them to do the right thing. Difficult, but not impossible.

Nobody needs to tell your daughter the obvious: She has many responsibilities—obligations to herself, to her family, to her community, to her school, and to her Creator. And which of these duties should take priority? The answer can be found in Matthew 6:33: "But seek first the kingdom of God and His righteousness, and all these things will be provided for you" (HCSB).

When your daughter "seeks first the kingdom of God," all the other obligations have a way of falling into place. And when your daughter learns the importance of honoring God with her time, her talents, and her prayers, she'll be much more likely to behave responsibly.

So do your daughter a favor: encourage her to take all her duties seriously, especially her duties to God. If she follows your advice, your child will soon discover that pleasing her Father in heaven isn't just the right thing to do; it's also the best way to live.

More from God's Word About Responsibility

But each person should examine his own work, and then he will have a reason for boasting in himself alone, and not in respect to someone else. For each person will have to carry his own load.

Galatians 6:4-5 HCSB

"Therefore I will judge you, O house of Israel, every one according to his ways," says the Lord God.

Ezekiel 18:30 NKJV

You will show me the path of life; in Your presence is fullness of joy; at Your right hand are pleasures forevermore.

Psalm 16:11 NKJV

We always pray for you that our God will consider you worthy of His calling, and will, by His power, fulfill every desire for goodness and the work of faith, so that the name of our Lord Jesus will be glorified by you, and you by Him, according to the grace of our God and the Lord Jesus Christ.

2 Thessalonians 1:11-12 HCSB

Therefore, get your minds ready for action, being self-disciplined, and set your hope completely on the grace to be brought to you at the revelation of Jesus Christ. As obedient children, do not be conformed to the desires of your former ignorance but, as the One who called you is holy, you also are to be holy in all your conduct.

1 Peter 1:13-15 HCSB

So then each of us shall give account of himself to God.

Romans 14:12 NKJV

For this very reason, make every effort to supplement your faith with goodness, goodness with knowledge, knowledge with self-control, self-control with endurance, endurance with godliness.

2 Peter 1:5-6 HCSB

Therefore as you have received Christ Jesus the Lord, walk in Him.

Colossians 2:6 HCSB

More Food for Thought About Responsibility

Jesus knows one of the greatest barriers to our faith is often our unwillingness to be made whole—our unwillingness to accept responsibility—our unwillingness to live without excuse for our spiritual smallness and immaturity.

Anne Graham Lotz

Whether we know it or not, whether we agree with it or not, whether we practice it or not, whether we like it or not, we are accountable to one another.

Charles Stanley

Although God causes all things to work together for good for His children, He still holds us accountable for our behavior.

Kay Arthur

God will take care of everything—the rest is up to you.

Lisa Whelchel

Action springs not from thought, but from a readiness for responsibility.

Dietrich Bonhoeffer

Our trustworthiness implies His trustworthiness.

Beth Moore

Living life with a consistent spiritual walk deeply influences those we love most.

Vonette Bright

What difference does it make to you what someone else becomes, or says, or does? You do not need to answer for others, only for yourself.

Thomas à Kempis

To walk out of His will is to walk into nowhere.

C. S. Lewis

GATHER YOUR THOUGHTS
Write Down at Least Three Things That
Your Daughter Needs to Hear
from You About Responsibility

_____

_____

_____

_____

_____

_____

_____

_____

_____

_____

_____

_____

_____

_____

Talk to Your Daughter About the Need to Serve

The greatest among you will be your servant.
Whoever exalts himself will be humbled,
and whoever humbles himself will be exalted.

Matthew 23:11-12 HCSB

If you and your family members genuinely seek to discover God's unfolding priorities for your lives, you must ask yourselves this question: "How does God want us to serve others?" And you may be certain of this: service to others is an integral part of God's plan for your lives, a plan that the Creator intends for you to impart to your daughter.

Christ was the ultimate servant, the Savior who gave His life for mankind. As His followers, we, too, must become humble servants. As Christians, we are clearly (and repeatedly) instructed to assist those in need. But, as weak human beings, we sometimes fall short as we seek to puff ourselves up and glorify our own accomplishments. Jesus commands otherwise. He teaches us that the most esteemed men and women are not the self-congratulatory leaders of society but are instead the humblest of servants.

Is your family willing to roll up its sleeves and become humble servants for Christ? Are you willing to do your part to make the world a better place? Are you willing to serve God now and trust Him to bless you later? The answer to these questions will determine the direction of your lives and the quality of your service.

As members of God's family, we must serve our neighbors quietly and without fanfare. We must find needs and meet them. We must lend helping hands and share kind words with humility in our hearts and praise on our lips. And we must remember that every time we help someone in need, we are serving our Savior . . . which, by the way, is precisely what we must do.

More from God's Word About Service

Worship the Lord your God and . . . serve Him only.

Matthew 4:10 HCSB

A person should consider us in this way: as servants of Christ and managers of God's mysteries. In this regard, it is expected of managers that each one be found faithful.

1 Corinthians 4:1-2 HCSB

If they serve Him obediently, they will end their days in prosperity and their years in happiness.

Job 36:11 HCSB

We must do the works of Him who sent Me while it is day. Night is coming when no one can work.

John 9:4 HCSB

Serve the Lord with gladness.

Psalm 100:2 HCSB

More Food for Thought About Service

God wants us to serve Him with a willing spirit, one that would choose no other way.

Beth Moore

No life can surpass that of a man who quietly continues to serve God in the place where providence has placed him.

C. H. Spurgeon

In the very place where God has put us, whatever its limitations, whatever kind of work it may be, we may indeed serve the Lord Christ.

Elisabeth Elliot

Through our service to others, God wants to influence our world for Him.

Vonette Bright

Service is the pathway to real significance.

Rick Warren

Christianity, in its purest form, is nothing more than seeing Jesus. Christian service, in its purest form, is nothing more than imitating him who we see. To see his Majesty and to imitate him: that is the sum of Christianity.

Max Lucado

So many times we say that we can't serve God because we aren't whatever is needed. We're not talented enough or smart enough or whatever. But if you are in covenant with Jesus Christ, He is responsible for covering your weaknesses, for being your strength. He will give you His abilities for your disabilities!

Kay Arthur

If you want to discover your spiritual gifts, start obeying God. As you serve Him, you will find that He has given you the gifts that are necessary to follow through in obedience.

Anne Graham Lotz

GATHER YOUR THOUGHTS
Write Down at Least Three Things That Your Daughter Needs to Hear from You About Service

_____

_____

_____

_____

_____

_____

_____

_____

_____

_____

_____

_____

_____

Talk to Your Daughter About the Power of Perseverance

*Though a righteous man falls seven times,
he will get up, but the wicked will stumble into ruin.*

Proverbs 24:16 HCSB

As she makes her way through life, your daughter will undoubtedly experience her fair share of disappointments, detours, false starts, and failures. Whenever she encounters one of life's dead ends, she'll face a test of character. So the question of the day is not if your daughter will be tested; it's how she will respond.

The old saying is as true today as it was when it was first spoken: "Life is a marathon, not a sprint." That's why wise travelers select a traveling companion who never tires and never falters. That partner, of course, is God.

The next time your daughter's courage is tested to the limit, remind her that God is always near and that the Creator offers strength and comfort to those who are wise enough to ask for it. Your daughter's job, of course, is to ask.

God operates on His own timetable, and sometimes He may answer your child's prayers with silence. But if your daughter remains steadfast, she may soon be surprised at the creative ways that God finds to help determined believers who possess the wisdom and the courage to persevere.

More from God's Word About Patience

We urge you, brethren, admonish the unruly, encourage the fainthearted, help the weak, be patient with everyone.

1 Thessalonians 5:14 NASB

Be completely humble and gentle; be patient, bearing with one another in love.

Ephesians 4:2 NIV

Yet the LORD longs to be gracious to you; he rises to show you compassion. For the LORD is a God of justice. Blessed are all who wait for him!

Isaiah 30:18 NIV

Wait on the LORD; Be of good courage, and He shall strengthen your heart; Wait, I say, on the LORD!

Psalm 27:14 NKJV

Let us not become weary in doing good, for at the proper time we will reap a harvest if we do not give up.

Galatians 6:9 NIV

Wherefore seeing we also are compassed about with so great a cloud of witnesses, let us lay aside every weight, and the sin which doth so easily beset us, and let us run with patience the race that is set before us . . . .

Hebrews 12:1 KJV

For you have need of endurance, so that when you have done the will of God, you may receive what was promised.

Hebrews 10:36 NASB

Thanks be to God! He gives us the victory through our Lord Jesus Christ. Therefore, my dear brothers, stand firm. Let nothing move you. Always give yourselves fully to the work of the Lord, because you know that your labor in the Lord is not in vain.

1 Corinthians 15:57-58 NIV

It is better to finish something than to start it. It is better to be patient than to be proud.

Ecclesiastes 7:8 NCV

More Food for Thought About Patience

Battles are won in the trenches, in the grit and grime of courageous determination; they are won day by day in the arena of life.

Charles Swindoll

You cannot persevere unless there is a trial in your life. There can be no victories without battles; there can be no peaks without valleys. If you want the blessing, you must be prepared to carry the burden and fight the battle. God has to balance privileges with responsibilities, blessings with burdens, or else you and I will become spoiled, pampered children.

Warren Wiersbe

Perseverance is more than endurance. It is endurance combined with absolute assurance and certainty that what we are looking for is going to happen.

Oswald Chambers

If things are tough, remember that every flower that ever bloomed had to go through a whole lot of dirt to get there.

Barbara Johnson

Only the man who follows the command of Jesus single-mindedly and unresistingly lets his yoke rest upon him, finds his burden easy, and under its gentle pressure receives the power to persevere in the right way.

Dietrich Bonhoeffer

Failure is one of life's most powerful teachers. How we handle our failures determines whether we're going to simply "get by" in life or "press on."

Beth Moore

By perseverance the snail reached the ark.

C. H. Spurgeon

Are you a Christian? If you are, how can you be hopeless? Are you so depressed by the greatness of your problems that you have given up all hope? Instead of giving up, would you patiently endure? Would you focus on Christ until you are so preoccupied with him alone that you fall prostrate before him?

Anne Graham Lotz

We are all on our way somewhere. We'll get there if we just keep going.

Barbara Johnson

GATHER YOUR THOUGHTS
Write Down at Least Three Things That
Your Daughter Needs to Hear
from You About Patience

Talk to Your Daughter About the Need to Stay Humble

Humble yourselves therefore under the mighty hand of God, so that He may exalt you in due time, casting all your care upon Him, because He cares about you.

1 Peter 5:6-7 HCSB

God's Word clearly instructs us to be humble. And that's good because, as fallible human beings, we have so very much to be humble about. Besides, God promises to bless the humble and correct the prideful. So why, then, are we humans so full of ourselves? The answer, of course, is that, if we are honest with ourselves and with our God, we simply can't be boastful; we should, instead, be eternally grateful and exceedingly humble. Yet humility is not, in most cases, a naturally occurring human trait.

Most of us are more than willing to overestimate our own accomplishments. We are tempted to say, "Look how wonderful I am!" . . . hoping all the while that the world will agree with our own self-appraisals. But those of us who fall prey to the sin of pride should beware—God is definitely not impressed by our prideful proclamations.

God honors humility . . . and He rewards those who humbly serve Him. So if you've acquired the wisdom to be humble, and if you're teaching your daughter to do likewise, you are to be congratulated. But if you've not yet overcome the tendency to overestimate your own accomplishments, or if your daughter seems overly impressed with her own accomplishments, then God still has some important (and perhaps painful) lessons to teach you—lessons about humility that you and your loved ones may still need to learn.

More from God's Word About
Giving God the Praise He Deserves

Praise the Lord, all nations! Glorify Him, all peoples! For great is His faithful love to us; the Lord's faithfulness endures forever. Hallelujah!

Psalm 117 HCSB

Therefore, through Him let us continually offer up to God a sacrifice of praise, that is, the fruit of our lips that confess His name.

Hebrews 13:15 HCSB

So that at the name of Jesus every knee should bow—of those who are in heaven and on earth and under the earth—and every tongue should confess that Jesus Christ is Lord, to the glory of God the Father.

Philippians 2:10-11 HCSB

Enter into his gates with thanksgiving, and into his courts with praise: be thankful unto him, and bless his name. For the LORD is good; his mercy is everlasting; and his truth endureth to all generations.

Psalm 100:4-5 KJV

Clothe yourselves with humility toward one another, because God resists the proud, but gives grace to the humble.

1 Peter 5:5 HCSB

But He said to me, "My grace is sufficient for you, for power is perfected in weakness." Therefore, I will most gladly boast all the more about my weaknesses, so that Christ's power may reside in me.

2 Corinthians 12:9 HCSB

You will save the humble people; but Your eyes are on the haughty, that You may bring them down.

2 Samuel 22:28 NKJV

If My people who are called by My name will humble them-selves, and pray and seek My face, and turn from their wicked ways, then I will hear from heaven, and will forgive their sin and heal their land.

2 Chronicles 7:14 NKJV

Do nothing out of rivalry or conceit, but in humility consider others as more important than yourselves.

Philippians 2:3 HCSB

More Food for Thought About Giving God the Praise He Deserves

If you know who you are in Christ, your personal ego is not an issue.

Beth Moore

Jesus had a humble heart. If He abides in us, pride will never dominate our lives.

Billy Graham

That's what I love about serving God. In His eyes, there are no little people . . . because there are no big people. We are all on the same playing field. We all start at square one. No one has it better than the other, or possesses unfair advantage.

Joni Eareckson Tada

One never can see, or not till long afterwards, why any one was selected for any job. And when one does, it is usually some reason that leaves no room for vanity.

C. S. Lewis

The great characteristic of the saint is humility.

Oswald Chambers

Let the love of Christ be believed in and felt in your hearts, and it will humble you.

C. H. Spurgeon

We are never stronger than the moment we admit we are weak.

Beth Moore

That some of my hymns have been dictated by the blessed Holy Spirit I have no doubt; and that others have been the result of deep meditation I know to be true; but that the poet has any right to claim special merit for himself is certainly presumptuous.

Fanny Crosby

All kindness and good deeds, we must keep silent. The result will be an inner reservoir of personality power.

Catherine Marshall

GATHER YOUR THOUGHTS
Write Down at Least Three Things That
Your Daughter Needs to Hear
from You About Humbling
Yourself Before God

Tell Your Daughter She Can Learn to Control the Direction of Her Thoughts

Finally brothers, whatever is true, whatever is honorable, whatever is just, whatever is pure, whatever is lovely, whatever is commendable—if there is any moral excellence and if there is any praise—dwell on these things.

Philippians 4:8 HCSB

Do you pay careful attention to the quality of your thoughts? And are you teaching your daughter to do likewise? Hopefully so, because the quality of your thoughts will help determine the quality of your lives.

Ours is a society that focuses on—and often glamorizes—the negative aspects of life. So both you and your daughter will be bombarded with messages—some subtle and some overt—that encourage you to think cynically about your circumstances, your world, and your faith. But God has other plans for you and your child.

God promises those who follow His Son can experience joyful abundance (John 10:10). Consequently, Christianity and pessimism simply don't mix. So if you find that your thoughts are being hijacked by the negativity that seems to have invaded our troubled world, it's time to focus less on your challenges and more on God's blessings.

God intends for you and your family members to experience joy and abundance, not cynicism and negativity. So, today and every day hereafter, celebrate the life that God has given you by focusing your thoughts upon those things that are worthy of praise. And while you're at it, teach your daughter to do the same. When you do, you'll both discover that God's gifts are simply too glorious, and too numerous, to count.

More from God's Word About
God's Blessings

You will show me the path of life; in Your presence is fullness of joy; at Your right hand are pleasures forevermore.

Psalm 16:11 NKJV

I will make them and the area around My hill a blessing: I will send down showers in their season—showers of blessing.

Ezekiel 34:26 HCSB

Obey My voice, and I will be your God, and you shall be my people. And walk in all the ways that I have commanded you, that it may be well with you.

Jeremiah 7:23 NKJV

The Lord bless you and keep you; the Lord make His face shine upon you, and be gracious to you.

Numbers 6:24-25 NKJV

Blessed is a man who endures trials, because when he passes the test he will receive the crown of life that He has promised to those who love Him.

James 1:12 HCSB

Set your minds on what is above, not on what is on the earth.

Colossians 3:2 HCSB

Commit your works to the Lord, and your thoughts will be established.

Proverbs 16:3 NKJV

Brothers, don't be childish in your thinking, but be infants in evil and adult in your thinking.

1 Corinthians 14:20 HCSB

Guard your heart above all else, for it is the source of life.

Proverbs 4:23 HCSB

May the words of my mouth and the meditation of my heart be acceptable to You, Lord, my rock and my Redeemer.

Psalm 19:14 HCSB

More Food for Thought About God's Blessings

Preoccupy my thoughts with your praise beginning today.

Joni Eareckson Tada

Every major spiritual battle is in the mind.

Charles Stanley

Attitude is the mind's paintbrush; it can color any situation.

Barbara Johnson

Your thoughts are the determining factor as to whose mold you are conformed to. Control your thoughts and you control the direction of your life.

Charles Stanley

As we have by faith said no to sin, so we should by faith say yes to God and set our minds on things above, where Christ is seated in the heavenlies.

Vonette Bright

Beware of cut-and-dried theologies that reduce the ways of God to a manageable formula that keeps life safe. God often does the unexplainable just to keep us on our toes—and also on our knees.

Warren Wiersbe

I became aware of one very important concept I had missed before: my attitude—not my circumstances—was what was making me unhappy.

Vonette Bright

No more imperfect thoughts. No more sad memories. No more ignorance. My redeemed body will have a redeemed mind. Grant me a foretaste of that perfect mind as you mirror your thoughts in me today.

Joni Eareckson Tada

The things we think are the things that feed our souls. If we think on pure and lovely things, we shall grow pure and lovely like them; and the converse is equally true.

Hannah Whitall Smith

GATHER YOUR THOUGHTS
Write Down at Least Three Things That
Your Daughter Needs to Hear
from You About God's Blessings

_____

_____

_____

_____

_____

_____

_____

_____

_____

_____

_____

_____

_____

Talk to Your Daughter About the Need to Obey the Golden Rule

*Therefore, whatever you want others to do for you,
do also the same for them—this is the Law and the Prophets.*

Matthew 7:12 HCSB

All over the world, loving parents preach the same lesson: kindness. And Christ taught that very same lesson when He spoke the words recorded in Matthew 7:12.

The Bible instructs us to be courteous and compassionate—and God's Word promises that when we follow these instructions, we are blessed. But sometimes, we fall short. Sometimes, amid the busyness and confusion of everyday life, we may neglect to share a kind word or a kind deed. This oversight hurts others, and it hurts us as well.

The Golden Rule commands us to treat others as we wish to be treated. When we weave the thread of kindness into the very fabric of our lives, we give glory to the One who gave His life for us.

Your daughter is growing up in a cynical society that often seems to focus on self-gratification and self-centeredness. Yet God's Word warns against becoming too attached to the world, and it's a warning that applies both to your daughter and to you.

So today, slow yourself down and be alert for those who need a smile, a kind word, or a helping hand. And encourage your daughter to do the same—encourage her to make kindness a centerpiece of her dealings with others. When she does, she'll discover that life is simply better when she treats other people in the same way she would want to be treated if she were in their shoes.

More from God's Word About Generosity

So let each one give as he purposes in his heart, not grudgingly or of necessity; for God loves a cheerful giver.

2 Corinthians 9:7 NKJV

Dear friend, you are showing your faith by whatever you do for the brothers, and this you are doing for strangers.

3 John 1:5 HCSB

In every way I've shown you that by laboring like this, it is necessary to help the weak and to keep in mind the words of the Lord Jesus, for He said, "It is more blessed to give than to receive."

Acts 20:35 HCSB

Bear one another's burdens, and so fulfill the law of Christ.

Galatians 6:2 NKJV

Love is patient; love is kind.

1 Corinthians 13:4 HCSB

If a brother or sister is without clothes and lacks daily food, and one of you says to them, "Go in peace, keep warm, and eat well," but you don't give them what the body needs, what good is it?

James 2:15–16 HCSB

Finally, all of you be of one mind, having compassion for one another; love as brothers, be tenderhearted, be courteous.

1 Peter 3:8 NKJV

And may the Lord make you increase and abound in love to one another and to all.

1 Thessalonians 3:12 NKJV

And be kind and compassionate to one another, forgiving one another, just as God also forgave you in Christ.

Ephesians 4:32 HCSB

Pure and undefiled religion before our God and Father is this: to look after orphans and widows in their distress and to keep oneself unstained by the world.

James 1:27 HCSB

More Food for Thought About Generosity

It is one of the most beautiful compensations of life that no one can sincerely try to help another without helping herself.

Barbara Johnson

The Golden Rule starts at home, but it should never stop there.

Marie T. Freeman

Choices can change our lives profoundly. The choice to mend a broken relationship, to say "yes" to a difficult assignment, to lay aside some important work to play with a child, to visit some forgotten person—these small choices may affect many lives eternally.

Gloria Gaither

Your light is the truth of the Gospel message itself as well as your witness as to Who Jesus is and what He has done for you. Don't hide it.

Anne Graham Lotz

In your desire to share the gospel, you may be the only Jesus someone else will ever meet. Be real and be involved with people.

Barbara Johnson

We must mirror God's love in the midst of a world full of hatred. We are the mirrors of God's love, so we may show Jesus by our lives.

Corrie ten Boom

In serving we uncover the greatest fulfillment within and become a stellar example of a woman who knows and loves Jesus.

Vonette Bright

God wants us to serve Him with a willing spirit, one that would choose no other way.

Beth Moore

Kindness in this world will do much to help others, not only to come into the light, but also to grow in grace day by day.

Fanny Crosby

GATHER YOUR THOUGHTS
Write Down at Least Three Things That Your Daughter Needs to Hear from You About Generosity

_____

_____

_____

_____

_____

_____

_____

_____

_____

_____

_____

_____

_____

_____

Talk to Your Daughter About the Dangers of Addiction

You shall have no other gods before Me.

Exodus 20:3 NKJV

Your daughter inhabits a society that glamorizes the use of drugs, alcohol, cigarettes, and other addictive substances. Why? The answer can be summed up in one word: money. Simply put, addictive substances are big money makers, so suppliers (of both legal and illegal substances) work overtime to make certain that youngsters like your daughter sample their products. Since the suppliers need a steady stream of new customers because the old ones are dying off (fast), they engage in a no-holds-barred struggle to find new users—or more accurately, new abusers.

The dictionary defines *addiction* as "the compulsive need for a habit-forming substance; the condition of being habitually and compulsively occupied with something." That definition is accurate, but incomplete. For Christians, addiction has an additional meaning: it means compulsively worshipping something other than God.

Your daughter may already know young people who are full-blown addicts, but with God's help she can avoid that fate. To do so, she should learn that addictive substances are, in truth, spiritual and emotional poisons. And she must avoid the temptation to experiment with addictive substances. If she can do these things, she will spare herself a lifetime of headaches and heartaches.

More from God's Word About
Abstinence, Moderation, and Virtue

Be sober! Be on the alert! Your adversary the Devil is prowling around like a roaring lion, looking for anyone he can devour.

1 Peter 5:8 HCSB

For we do not have a High Priest who cannot sympathize with our weaknesses, but was in all points tempted as we are, yet without sin. Let us therefore come boldly to the throne of grace, that we may obtain mercy and find grace to help in time of need.

Hebrews 4:15-16 NKJV

Jesus responded, "I assure you: Everyone who commits sin is a slave of sin."

John 8:34 HCSB

Death is the reward of an undisciplined life; your foolish decisions trap you in a dead end.

Proverbs 5:23 MSG

Yet in all these things we are more than conquerors through Him who loved us.

Romans 8:37 NKJV

More Food for Thought About
Abstinence, Moderation, Virtue, and God

Virtue—even attempted virtue—brings light; indulgence brings fog.

C. S. Lewis

To many, total abstinence is easier than perfect moderation.

St. Augustine

God is able to take mistakes, when they are committed to Him, and make of them something for our good and for His glory.

Ruth Bell Graham

No matter how crazy or nutty your life has seemed, God can make something strong and good out of it. He can help you grow wide branches for others to use as shelter.

Barbara Johnson

Nobody is good by accident. No man ever became holy by chance.

C. H. Spurgeon

A live body is not one that never gets hurt, but one that can to some extent repair itself. In the same way a Christian is not a man who never goes wrong, but a man who is enabled to repent and pick himself up and begin over again after each stumble—because the Christ-life is inside him, repairing him all the time, enabling him to repeat (in some degree) the kind of voluntary death which Christ himself carried out.

C. S. Lewis

When we face an impossible situation, all self-reliance and self-confidence must melt away; we must be totally dependent on Him for the resources.

Anne Graham Lotz

A person may not be responsible for his last drink, but he certainly was for the first.

Billy Graham

Addiction is the most powerful psychic enemy of humanity's desire for God.

Gerald May

GATHER YOUR THOUGHTS
Write Down at Least Three Things That Your Daughter Needs to Hear from You About Abstinence, Moderation, Virtue, and God

_____

_____

_____

_____

_____

_____

_____

_____

_____

_____

_____

_____

_____

Talk to Your Daughter About the Relative *Unimportance* of Appearance

The LORD doesn't make decisions the way you do!
People judge by outward appearance,
but the LORD looks at a person's thoughts and intentions.

1 Samuel 16:7 NLT

Because your daughter lives in a society that places great emphasis on physical appearance, she will be tempted to grade herself, first and foremost, on her looks. She may focus on her weight, her clothes, her hair, or some other aspect of her physical appearance. But if that's her primary focus, she's making a big mistake, a mistake that you can help her rectify.

As a thoughtful parent, it's up to you to remind your child that her first obligation is to please God, not her friends. You should remind her that while the world sees her as she appears to be, God sees her as she really is. And it's His opinion that really matters.

Perhaps you've already discovered that few things in life are more futile than "keeping up appearances," but your daughter may not yet be mature enough to understand the dangers of excessive people-pleasing. After all, the media is trying to convince your daughter that her happiness depends on the color of her hair or the condition of her wardrobe or her dress size. But nothing could be further from the truth.

So as you're talking to your daughter, remind her to please God first, not society, not peers, and not friends. When she does, she will be blessed today, tomorrow, and forever.

More from God's Word About Pleasing Him, Not People

Your beauty should not come from outward adornment, such as braided hair and the wearing of gold jewelry and fine clothes. Instead, it should be that of your inner self, the unfading beauty of a gentle and quiet spirit, which is of great worth in God's sight.

1 Peter 3:3-4 NIV

He has made everything beautiful in its time.

Ecclesiastes 3:11 NIV

If you decide for God, living a life of God-worship, it follows that you don't fuss about what's on the table at mealtimes or whether the clothes in your closet are in fashion. There is far more to your life than the food you put in your stomach, more to your outer appearance than the clothes you hang on your body.

Matthew 6:25 MSG

And let the beauty of the Lord our God be upon us.

Psalm 90:17 NKJV

Your heart will be where your treasure is.

Luke 12:34 NCV

More Food for Thought About Pleasing God, Not People

Outside appearances, things like the clothes you wear or the car you drive, are important to other people but totally unimportant to God. Trust God.

Marie T. Freeman

If the narrative of the Scriptures teaches us anything, from the serpent in the Garden to the carpenter in Nazareth, it teaches us that things are rarely what they seem, that we shouldn't be fooled by appearances.

John Eldredge

The single most important element in any human relationship is honesty—with oneself, with God, and with others.

Catherine Marshall

Don't be addicted to approval. Follow your heart. Do what you believe God is telling you to do, and stand firm in Him and Him alone.

Joyce Meyer

Our ultimate aim in life is not to be healthy, wealthy, prosperous, or problem free. Our ultimate aim in life is to bring glory to God.

Anne Graham Lotz

Once you loosen up, let yourself be who you are: the wonderful, witty woman whom God will use to encourage and uplift other people.

Barbara Johnson

A balanced woman of God sees herself as valuable, gifted, responsible for her own growth and maturity—not overly dependent on anyone to get her through life or to make her secure.

Charles Swindoll

Being loved by Him whose opinion matters most gives us the security to risk loving, too—even loving ourselves.

Gloria Gaither

GATHER YOUR THOUGHTS
Write Down at Least Three Things That
Your Daughter Needs to Hear
from You About Pleasing God,
Not People

Remind Your Daughter to Choose Her Friends Wisely

Do not be deceived:
"Bad company corrupts good morals."
1 Corinthians 15:33 HCSB

Peer pressure can be a good thing or a bad thing for your daughter, depending upon her peers. If her peers encourage her to make integrity a habit—if they encourage her to follow God's will and to obey God's commandments—your daughter will experience positive peer pressure, and that's good.

But, if your youngster becomes involved with people who encourage her to do foolish things, she'll face a different kind of peer pressure. If your daughter feels pressured to do things or to say things that lead her away from God, she's aiming straight for trouble.

As you talk to your child about the differences between positive and negative peer pressure, here are a few things to emphasize:

1. Peer pressure exists, and your daughter will experience it.
2. If your daughter's friends encourage her to honor God and become a better person, peer pressure can be a good thing.
3. If your daughter's friends encourage her to misbehave or underachieve, that sort of peer pressure is destructive.
4. When peer pressure turns negative, it's up to your daughter to start finding new friends. Today.

To sum it up, your daughter has a choice: she can choose to please God first, or she can fall prey to negative peer pressure. The choice is hers—and so are the consequences.

More from God's Word About Peer Pressure

He who walks with wise men will be wise, but the companion of fools will be destroyed.

Proverbs 13:20 NKJV

For am I now trying to win the favor of people, or God? Or am I striving to please people? If I were still trying to please people, I would not be a slave of Christ.

Galatians 1:10 HCSB

My son, if sinners entice you, don't be persuaded.

Proverbs 1:10 HCSB

Blessed is the man who walks not in the counsel of the ungodly, nor stands in the path of sinners, nor sits in the seat of the scornful; but his delight is in the law of the Lord, and in His law he meditates day and night.

Psalm 1:1-2 NKJV

More Food for Thought About
Peer Pressure

You will get untold flak for prioritizing God's revealed and present will for your life over man's . . . but, boy, is it worth it.

Beth Moore

We, as God's people, are not only to stay far away from sin and sinners who would entice us, but we are to be so like our God that we mourn over sin.

Kay Arthur

It is impossible to please everybody. It's not impossible to please God. So try pleasing God.

Marie T. Freeman

True friends will always lift you higher and challenge you to walk in a manner pleasing to our Lord.

Lisa Bevere

If I had to advise parents, I should tell them to take great care about the people with whom their children associate. Much harm may result from bad company, and we are inclined by nature to follow the worse rather than the better.

Elizabeth Ann Seton

If you choose to awaken a passion for God, you will have to choose your friends wisely.

Lisa Bevere

It is comfortable to know that we are responsible to God and not to man. It is a small matter to be judged of man's judgement.

Lottie Moon

Comparison is the root of all feelings of inferiority.

James Dobson

GATHER YOUR THOUGHTS
Write Down at Least Three Things That
Your Daughter Needs to Hear
from You About Peer Pressure

_____

_____

_____

_____

_____

_____

_____

_____

_____

_____

_____

_____

_____

Remind Your Daughter That Tough Times Don't Last Forever but God's Love Does

God blesses the people who patiently endure testing.
Afterward they will receive the crown of life
that God has promised to those who love him.

James 1:12 NLT

Every human life (including your daughter's) is a tapestry of events: some grand, some not-so-grand, and some downright disheartening. When your child reaches the mountaintops of life, she'll find that praising God is easy. But, when the storm clouds form overhead and she finds herself in the dark valleys of life, her faith will be stretched, sometimes to the breaking point.

As Christians, we can be comforted: Wherever we find ourselves, whether at the top of the mountain or the depths of the valley, God is there, and because He cares for us, we can live courageously.

The Bible promises this: tough times are temporary but God's love is not—God's love lasts forever. Psalm 147 promises, "He heals the brokenhearted and binds up their wounds" (v. 3, HCSB), but Psalm 147 doesn't say that He heals them instantly. Usually, it takes time (and effort) to fix things.

So your daughter should learn that when she faces tough times, she should face them with God by her side. Your daughter should understand that when she encounters setbacks—and she will—she should always ask for God's help. And your daughter should learn to be patient. God will work things out, just as He has promised, but He will do it in His own way and in His own time.

More from God's Word About Adversity

When you are in distress and all these things have happened to you, you will return to the Lord your God in later days and obey Him. He will not leave you, destroy you, or forget the covenant with your fathers that He swore to them by oath, because the Lord your God is a compassionate God.

Deuteronomy 4:30-31 HCSB

Whatever has been born of God conquers the world. This is the victory that has conquered the world: our faith.

1 John 5:4 HCSB

Dear friends, when the fiery ordeal arises among you to test you, don't be surprised by it, as if something unusual were happening to you. Instead, as you share in the sufferings of the Messiah rejoice, so that you may also rejoice with great joy at the revelation of His glory.

1 Peter 4:12-13 HCSB

I called to the Lord in my distress; I called to my God. From His temple He heard my voice.

2 Samuel 22:7 HCSB

More Food for Thought About Adversity

God will never let you sink under your circumstances. He always provides a safety net and His love always encircles.

Barbara Johnson

If you learn to trust God with a child-like dependence on Him as your loving Heavenly Father, no trouble can destroy you.

Billy Graham

God whispers to us in our pleasures, speaks in our conscience, but shouts in our pain.

C. S. Lewis

The sermon of your life in tough times ministers to people more powerfully than the most eloquent speaker.

Bill Bright

Measure the size of the obstacles against the size of God.

Beth Moore

Adversity is not simply a tool. It is God's most effective tool for the advancement of our spiritual lives. The circumstances and events that we see as setbacks are oftentimes the very things that launch us into periods of intense spiritual growth. Once we begin to understand this, and accept it as a spiritual fact of life, adversity becomes easier to bear.

Charles Stanley

Faith is a strong power, mastering any difficulty in the strength of the Lord who made heaven and earth.

Corrie ten Boom

If all struggles and sufferings were eliminated, the spirit would no more reach maturity than would the child.

Elisabeth Elliot

Often the trials we mourn are really gateways into the good things we long for.

Hannah Whitall Smith

GATHER YOUR THOUGHTS
Write Down at Least Three Things That Your Daughter Needs to Hear from You About Adversity

_____

_____

_____

_____

_____

_____

_____

_____

_____

_____

_____

_____

_____

Tell Your Daughter That Since Opportunities Are Everywhere, She Should Keep Her Eyes and Her Heart Open

Therefore, as we have opportunity,
we must work for the good of all, especially for those
who belong to the household of faith.

Galatians 6:10 HCSB

Because we are saved by a risen Christ, we can have hope for the future, no matter how troublesome our present circumstances may seem. After all, God has promised that we are His throughout eternity. And, He has told us that we must place our trust in Him.

Of course, we will face disappointments and failures while we are here on earth, but these are only temporary defeats. Of course, this world can be a place of trials and tribulations, but when we place our trust in the Giver of all things good, we are secure. God has promised us peace, joy, and eternal life. And God keeps His promises.

Whether you realize it or not, opportunities are whirling around you and your family like stars crossing the night sky: beautiful to observe, but too numerous to count. Yet you may be too concerned with the challenges of everyday living to notice those opportunities. That's why you should slow down occasionally, catch your breath, and focus your thoughts on two things: the talents and the opportunities that God has placed before you and your loved ones. God is leading you and your family in the direction of those opportunities. Your task is to watch carefully, to pray fervently, and to act accordingly.

More from God's Word About Opportunity

You will show me the path of life; in Your presence is fullness of joy; at Your right hand are pleasures forevermore.

Psalm 16:11 NKJV

For I know the thoughts that I think toward you, says the Lord, thoughts of peace and not of evil, to give you a future and a hope. Then you will call upon Me and go and pray to Me, and I will listen to you.

Jeremiah 29:11-12 NKJV

But Jesus looked at them and said, "With men this is impossible, but with God all things are possible."

Matthew 19:26 HCSB

For God has not given us a spirit of fearfulness, but one of power, love, and sound judgment.

2 Timothy 1:7 HCSB

I am able to do all things through Him who strengthens me.

Philippians 4:13 HCSB

More Food for Thought About Opportunity

There is no limit to what God can make us—if we are willing.

Oswald Chambers

We are all faced with a series of great opportunities, brilliantly disguised as unsolvable problems. Unsolvable without God's wisdom, that is.

Charles Swindoll

Every day we live is a priceless gift of God, loaded with possibilities to learn something new, to gain fresh insights.

Dale Evans Rogers

God specializes in things fresh and firsthand. His plans for you this year may outshine those of the past. He's prepared to fill your days with reasons to give Him praise.

Joni Eareckson Tada

With the right attitude and a willingness to pay the price, almost anyone can pursue nearly any opportunity and achieve it.

John Maxwell

He who waits until circumstances completely favor his undertaking will never accomplish anything.

Martin Luther

Life is a glorious opportunity.

Billy Graham

Great opportunities often disguise themselves in small tasks.

Rick Warren

God surrounds you with opportunity. You and I are free in Jesus Christ, not to do whatever we want, but to be all that God wants us to be.

Warren Wiersbe

GATHER YOUR THOUGHTS
Write Down at Least Three Things That
Your Daughter Needs to Hear
from You About Opportunity

Talk to Your Daughter About the Need to Manage Money Wisely

*Good planning and hard work lead to prosperity,
but hasty shortcuts lead to poverty.*

Proverbs 21:5 NLT

A s a parent, you know, from firsthand experience, that the job of raising your daughter is an immense responsibility. And one of your parental duties is to teach her how to manage money.

If you're serious about helping your daughter become a savvy spender and a serious saver, you must teach by example. After all, parental pronouncements are far easier to make than they are to live by. Yet your daughter will likely learn far more from your actions than from your words. So please remember that in matters of money, you are not just a role model; you are *the* role model. And as you begin to teach your child a few common-sense principles about spending and saving, remember that your actions will speak far more loudly than your words.

The world won't protect your daughter from the consequences of frivolous spending, and neither should you. So if she overspends, don't be too quick to bail her out of her troubles. As a parent, your job is not necessarily to protect your youngster from pain, but to ensure that she learns from the consequences of her actions.

Thankfully, the basic principles of money management aren't very hard to understand. These principles can be summed up in three simple steps: 1. Have a budget and live by it, spending less than you make; 2. Save and invest wisely; 3. Give God His fair share. These steps are so straightforward that even a young child can grasp them, so you need not have attended business school (or seminary) to teach powerful lessons about faith and finances. And that's good because your daughter needs your sound advice and your good example . . . but not necessarily in that order.

More from God's Word About Financial Common Sense

For I am the Lord, I do not change. Will a man rob God? Yet you have robbed Me! But you say, in what way have we robbed You? In tithes and offerings. You are cursed with a curse, for you have robbed Me, even this whole nation. Bring all the tithes into the storehouse, that there may be food in My house.

Malachi 3:6, 8-10 NKJV

And my God shall supply all your need according to His riches in glory by Christ Jesus.

Philippians 4:19 NKJV

Commit your activities to the Lord and your plans will be achieved.

Proverbs 16:3 HCSB

Based on the gift they have received, everyone should use it to serve others, as good managers of the varied grace of God.

1 Peter 4:10 HCSB

More Food for Thought About Financial Common Sense

Jesus had much to say about money, . . . more than about almost any other subject.

Bill Bright

Sadly, family problems and even financial problems are seldom the real problem, but often the symptom of a weak or nonexistent value system.

Dave Ramsey

Here's a good recipe for managing your money: Never make a big financial decision without first talking it over with God.

Marie T. Freeman

There is nothing wrong with asking God's direction. But it is wrong to go our own way, then expect Him to bail us out.

Larry Burkett

Often, our character is at greater risk in prosperity than in adversity.

Beth Moore

As faithful stewards of what we have, ought we not to give earnest thought to our staggering surplus?

Elisabeth Elliot

It is easy to determine the importance money plays in God's plan by the abundance of Scripture that relates to it—more than seven hundred verses directly refer to its use.

Larry Burkett

There is no way to draw closer to God unless you are in the Word of God every day. It's your compass. Your guide. You can't get where you need to go without it.

Stormie Omartian

GATHER YOUR THOUGHTS
Write Down at Least Three Things That
Your Daughter Needs to Hear
from You About Financial
Common Sense

_____

_____

_____

_____

_____

_____

_____

_____

_____

_____

_____

_____

_____

Talk to Your Daughter About Her Physical Health

Therefore, brothers, by the mercies of God,
I urge you to present your bodies as a living sacrifice,
holy and pleasing to God; this is your spiritual worship.

Romans 12:1 HCSB

I n the Book of Romans, Paul encourages us to make our bodies "holy and pleasing to God." Paul adds that to do so is a "spiritual act of worship." For believers, the implication is clear: God intends that we take special care of the bodies He has given us. But it's tempting to do otherwise.

We live in a fast-food world where unhealthy choices are convenient, inexpensive, and tempting. And, we live in a digital world filled with modern conveniences that often rob us of the physical exercise needed to maintain healthy lifestyles. As a result, too many of us, adults and children alike, find ourselves glued to the television, with a snack in one hand and a clicker in the other. The results are as unfortunate as they are predictable.

As adults, each of us bears a personal responsibility for the general state of our own physical health. Certainly, various aspects of health are beyond our control: illness sometimes strikes even the healthiest people. But for most of us, physical health is a choice: it is the result of hundreds of small decisions that we make every day of our lives. If we make decisions that promote good health, our bodies respond. But if we fall into bad habits and undisciplined lifestyles, we suffer tragic consequences.

When our unhealthy habits lead to poor health, we find it all too easy to look beyond ourselves and assign blame. In fact, we live in a society where blame has become a national obsession: we blame cigarette manufacturers, restaurants, and food producers, to name only a few. But to blame others is to miss the point: We, and we alone, are responsible for the way that we treat our bodies. And the sooner that we accept that responsibility, the sooner we can assert control over our bodies and our lives.

Do you sincerely desire to improve your physical health? And do you wish to encourage your child to do likewise? If so, start by taking personal responsibility for the body that God has given you. Next, be sure to teach your daughter the common-sense lessons of a sensible diet and regular exercise. Then, make a solemn pledge to yourself that you'll help your family make the choices that are necessary to enjoy longer, healthier, happier lives. No one can make those choices for you; you must make them for yourselves.

More from God's Word About Health

Don't you know that you are God's sanctuary and that the Spirit of God lives in you?

1 Corinthians 3:16 HCSB

For it was You who created my inward parts; You knit me together in my mother's womb. I will praise You, because I have been remarkably and wonderfully made.

Psalm 139:13-14 HCSB

More Food for Thought About Health

God wants you to give Him your body. Some people do foolish things with their bodies. God wants your body as a holy sacrifice.

Warren Wiersbe

The key to healthy eating is moderation and managing what you eat every day.

John Maxwell

Our primary motivation should not be for more energy or to avoid a heart attack but to please God with our bodies.

Carole Lewis

Most people I know either love exercise and do it excessively, or they hate it and avoid it completely; yet consistent exercise is one of the keys to good health.

John Maxwell

You can't buy good health at the doctor's office—you've got to earn it for yourself.

Marie T. Freeman

People are funny. When they are young, they will spend their health to get wealth. Later, they will gladly pay all they have trying to get their health back.

John Maxwell

Ultimate healing and the glorification of the body are certainly among the blessings of Calvary for the believing Christian. Immediate healing is not guaranteed.

Warren Wiersbe

Exercise and physical fitness have a cause-and-effect relationship; fitness comes as a direct result of regular, sustained, and intense exercise.

John Maxwell

GATHER YOUR THOUGHTS
Write Down at Least Three Things That
Your Daughter Needs to Hear
from You About Health

_____

_____

_____

_____

_____

_____

_____

_____

_____

_____

_____

_____

_____

_____

Temptations Are Everywhere, So Guard Your Heart and Mind

My son, if sinners entice you, don't be persuaded.

Proverbs 1:10 HCSB

Because our world is filled with temptations, your daughter will encounter them at every turn. The devil, it seems, is working overtime these days, causing heartache in more places and in more ways than ever before. So your daughter must remain vigilant. How? By avoiding those places where Satan can most easily tempt her and by arming herself with God's Holy Word.

After fasting forty days and nights in the desert, Jesus Himself was tempted by Satan. Christ used Scripture to rebuke the devil (Matthew 4:1-11). We must do likewise. The Holy Bible provides us with a perfect blueprint for righteous living. If we consult that blueprint each day and follow its instructions carefully, we build our lives according to God's plan. And when we do, we are secure.

Your child lives in a society that encourages her to "try" any number of things that are dangerous to her spiritual, mental, or physical health. It's a world brimming with traps and temptations designed to corrupt her character, ruin her health, sabotage her relationships, and derail her future. Your job, as a thoughtful parent, is to warn your daughter of these dangers . . . and to keep warning her.

More from God's Word About
Guarding Against Evil

Above all else, guard your heart, for it affects everything you do.

Proverbs 4:23 NLT

The peace of God, which surpasses all understanding, will guard your hearts and minds through Christ Jesus.

Philippians 4:7 NKJV

Don't copy the behavior and customs of this world, but let God transform you into a new person by changing the way you think. Then you will know what God wants you to do, and you will know how good and pleasing and perfect his will really is.

Romans 12:2 NLT

Do not fret because of evildoers; don't envy the wicked.

Proverbs 24:19 NLT

Therefore, submit to God. But resist the Devil, and he will flee from you. Draw near to God, and He will draw near to you. Cleanse your hands, sinners, and purify your hearts, double-minded people!

James 4:7-8 HCSB

No temptation has overtaken you except what is common to humanity. God is faithful and He will not allow you to be tempted beyond what you are able, but with the temptation He will also provide a way of escape, so that you are able to bear it.

1 Corinthians 10:13 HCSB

Be sober! Be on the alert! Your adversary the Devil is prowling around like a roaring lion, looking for anyone he can devour.

1 Peter 5:8 HCSB

Put on the full armor of God so that you can stand against the tactics of the Devil.

Ephesians 6:11 HCSB

Stay awake and pray, so that you won't enter into temptation. The spirit is willing, but the flesh is weak.

Matthew 26:41 HCSB

The Spirit's law of life in Christ Jesus has set you free from the law of sin and of death.

Romans 8:2 HCSB

More Food for Thought About Guarding Against Evil

It is easier to stay out of temptation than to get out of it.

Rick Warren

There is sharp necessity for giving Christ absolute obedience. The devil bids for our complete self-will. To whatever extent we give this self-will the right to be master over our lives, we are, to an extent, giving Satan a toehold.

Catherine Marshall

Instant intimacy is one of the leading warning signals of a seduction.

Beth Moore

Lord, what joy to know that Your powers are so much greater than those of the enemy.

Corrie ten Boom

Deception is the enemy's ongoing plan of attack.

Stormie Omartian

Flee temptation without leaving a forwarding address.

Barbara Johnson

The Bible teaches us in times of temptation there is one command: Flee! Get away from it, for every struggle against lust using only one's own strength is doomed to failure.

Dietrich Bonhoeffer

Many times the greatest temptations confront us when we are in the center of the will of God, because being there has offset and frustrated Satans' methods of attack.

Franklin Graham

Temptation is not a sin. Even Jesus was tempted. The Lord Jesus gives you the strength needed to resist temptation.

Corrie ten Boom

GATHER YOUR THOUGHTS
Write Down at Least Three Things That Your Daughter Needs to Hear from You About Guarding Against Evil

Remind Your Daughter to Keep Her Problems in Proper Perspective

*Set your minds on what is above,
not on what is on the earth.*
Colossians 3:2 HCSB

For parents and kids alike, life is busy and complicated. Amid the rush and crush of the daily grind, it is easy to lose perspective . . . easy, but wrong. When our world seems to be spinning out of control, we can regain perspective by slowing down long enough to put things in proper perspective. But slowing down isn't always easy, especially for young people. So your daughter may, on occasion, become convinced (wrongly) that today's problems are both permanent and catastrophic. And if she starts making mountains out of molehills, it's up to you, as a thoughtful parent, to teach her how to regain perspective.

When you have a problem that seems overwhelming, do you carve out quiet moments to think about God's promises and what those promises mean in the grand scope of eternity? Are you wise enough to offer thanksgiving and praise to your Creator, in good times and bad? And do you encourage your daughter to do the same? If so, your child will be blessed by your instruction and your example.

The familiar words of Psalm 46:10 remind us to "Be still, and know that I am God" (NKJV). When we do so, we encounter the awesome presence of our Heavenly Father. But, when we ignore the presence of our Creator, we rob ourselves of His perspective, His peace, and His joy.

So today and every day, make time to be still before the Creator, and encourage your daughter to do likewise. Then, both of you can face life's inevitable setbacks—all of which, by the way, are temporary setbacks—with the wisdom and power that only God can provide.

More from God's Word About Wisdom

Don't abandon wisdom, and she will watch over you; love her, and she will guard you.

Proverbs 4:6 HCSB

Acquire wisdom—how much better it is than gold! And acquire understanding—it is preferable to silver.

Proverbs 16:16 HCSB

The one who acquires good sense loves himself; one who safeguards understanding finds success.

Proverbs 19:8 HCSB

Let no one deceive himself. If anyone among you seems to be wise in this age, let him become a fool that he may become wise. For the wisdom of this world is foolishness with God. For it is written, "He catches the wise in their own craftiness."

1 Corinthians 3:18-19 NKJV

Who is wise and understanding among you? Let him show by good conduct that his works are done in the meekness of wisdom.

James 3:13 NKJV

Now if any of you lacks wisdom, he should ask God, who gives to all generously and without criticizing, and it will be given to him.

James 1:5 HCSB

Pay careful attention, then, to how you walk—not as unwise people but as wise.

Ephesians 5:15 HCSB

For now we see in a mirror, dimly, but then face to face. Now I know in part, but then I shall know just as I also am known.

1 Corinthians 13:12 NKJV

The Lord says, "I will make you wise and show you where to go. I will guide you and watch over you."

Psalm 32:8 NCV

More Food for Thought About Wisdom

Life: the time God gives you to determine how you spend eternity.

Anonymous

As you and I lay up for ourselves living, lasting treasures in Heaven, we come to the awesome conclusion that we ourselves are His treasure!

Anne Graham Lotz

Salvation involves so much more than knowing facts about Jesus Christ, or even having special feelings toward Jesus Christ. Salvation comes to us when, by an act of will, we receive Christ as our Savior and Lord.

Warren Wiersbe

We are always trying to "find ourselves" when that is exactly what we need to lose.

Vance Havner

Going to church does not make you a Christian anymore than going to McDonald's makes you a hamburger.

Anonymous

All that is not eternal is eternally out of date.

C. S. Lewis

I now know the power of the risen Lord! He lives! The dawn of Easter has broken in my own soul! My night is gone!

Mrs. Charles E. Cowman

The crucial question for each of us is this: What do you think of Jesus, and do you yet have a personal acquaintance with Him?

Hannah Whitall Smith

God is in control, and therefore in everything I can give thanks, not because of the situation, but because of the One who directs and rules over it.

Kay Arthur

GATHER YOUR THOUGHTS
Write Down at Least Three Things That Your Daughter Needs to Hear from You About Wisdom

MOTHER-DAUGHTER CONVERSATION #29

Talk to Your Daughter About Her Very Bright Future

There is surely a future hope for you,
and your hope will not be cut off.

Proverbs 23:18 NIV

The hope that the world offers is fleeting and imperfect. The hope that God offers is unchanging, unshakable, and unending. It is no wonder, then, that when we seek security from worldly sources, our hopes are often dashed. Thankfully, God has no such record of failure.

Because we are saved by a risen Christ, we can have hope for the future, no matter how troublesome our present circumstances may seem. After all, God has promised that we are His throughout eternity. And, He has told us that we must place our hopes in Him.

All of us, parents and children alike, will face disappointments and failures while we are here on earth, but these are only temporary defeats. Of course, this world can be a place of trials and tribulations, but when we place our trust in the Giver of all things good, we are secure. God has promised us peace, joy, and eternal life. And God keeps His promises today, tomorrow, and forever.

Are you willing to place your future in the hands of a loving and all-knowing God? Will you face today's challenges with optimism and hope? And will you encourage your daughter to do the same? Hopefully, you can answer these questions with a resounding yes. After all, God created you and your child for very important purposes: His purposes. And you both still have important work to do: His work.

So today, as you live in the present and look to the future, remember that God has a plan for you and your daughter. And it's up to both of you to act—and to believe—accordingly.

More from God's Word About Future and Hope

Be of good courage, and he shall strengthen your heart, all ye that hope in the LORD.

Psalm 31:24 KJV

The Lord is good to those whose hope is in him, to the one who seeks him; it is good to wait quietly for the salvation of the Lord.

Lamentations 3:25-26 NIV

Blessed is he whose help is the God of Jacob, whose hope is in the LORD his God, the Maker of heaven and earth, the sea, and everything in them—the LORD, who remains faithful forever.

Psalm 146:5-6 NIV

May the God of hope fill you with all joy and peace as you trust in him, so that you may overflow with hope by the power of the Holy Spirit.

Romans 15:13 NIV

More Food for Thought About
Future and Hope

You can look forward with hope, because one day there will be no more separation, no more scars, and no more suffering in My Father's House. It's the home of your dreams!

Anne Graham Lotz

The future lies all before us. Shall it only be a slight advance upon what we usually do? Ought it not to be a bound, a leap forward to altitudes of endeavor and success undreamed of before?

Annie Armstrong

Every saint has a past—every sinner has a future!

Anonymous

Allow your dreams a place in your prayers and plans. God-given dreams can help you move into the future He is preparing for you.

Barbara Johnson

The Christian believes in a fabulous future.

Billy Graham

Every experience God gives us, every person he brings into our lives, is the perfect preparation for the future that only he can see.

Corrie ten Boom

Take courage. We walk in the wilderness today and in the Promised Land tomorrow.

D. L. Moody

It may be that the day of judgment will dawn tomorrow; in that case, we shall gladly stop working for a better tomorrow. But not before.

Dietrich Bonhoeffer

Our future may look fearfully intimidating, yet we can look up to the Engineer of the Universe, confident that nothing escapes His attention or slips out of the control of those strong hands.

Elisabeth Elliot

GATHER YOUR THOUGHTS
Write Down at Least Three Things That
Your Daughter Needs to Hear
from You About the Future
and Hope

Talk to Your Daughter About God's Gift of Eternal Life

> *"I assure you: Anyone who hears My word and believes Him who sent Me has eternal life and will not come under judgment, but has passed from death to life."*
>
> John 5:24–25 HCSB

Eternal life is not an event that begins when we die. Eternal life begins when we invite Jesus into our hearts. The moment we allow Jesus to reign over our hearts, we've already begun our eternal journeys.

As a thoughtful Christian parent, it's important to remind your child that God's plans are not limited to the ups and downs of everyday life. In fact, the ups and downs of the daily grind are, quite often, impossible for us to understand. As mere mortals, our understanding of the present and our visions for the future—like our lives here on earth—are limited. God's vision is not burdened by such limitations: His plans extend throughout all eternity. And we must trust Him even when we cannot understand the particular details of His plan.

So let us praise the Creator for His priceless gift, and let us share the Good News with all who cross our paths. We return our Father's love by accepting His grace and by sharing His message and His love. When we do, we are blessed here on earth and throughout all eternity.

More from God's Word About
Eternal Life

And this is the testimony: God has given us eternal life, and this life is in His Son. The one who has the Son has life. The one who doesn't have the Son of God does not have life.

1 John 5:11-12 HCSB

We do not want you to be uninformed, brothers, concerning those who are asleep, so that you will not grieve like the rest, who have no hope. Since we believe that Jesus died and rose again, in the same way God will bring with Him those who have fallen asleep through Jesus.

1 Thessalonians 4:13-14 HCSB

Jesus said to her, "I am the resurrection and the life. The one who believes in Me, even if he dies, will live. Everyone who lives and believes in Me will never die—ever. Do you believe this?"

John 11:25-26 HCSB

Pursue righteousness, godliness, faith, love, endurance, and gentleness. Fight the good fight for the faith; take hold of eternal life, to which you were called and have made a good confession before many witnesses.

1 Timothy 6:11-12 HCSB

More Food for Thought About Eternal Life

Your choice to either receive or reject the Lord Jesus Christ will determine where you spend eternity.

Anne Graham Lotz

If you are a believer, your judgment will not determine your eternal destiny. Christ's finished work on Calvary was applied to you the moment you accepted Christ as Savior.

Beth Moore

I can still hardly believe it. I, with shriveled, bent fingers, atrophied muscles, gnarled knees, and no feeling from the shoulders down, will one day have a new body—light, bright and clothed in righteousness—powerful and dazzling.

Joni Eareckson Tada

Teach us to set our hopes on heaven, to hold firmly to the promise of eternal life, so that we can withstand the struggles and storms of this world.

Max Lucado

God has promised us abundance, peace, and eternal life. These treasures are ours for the asking; all we must do is claim them. One of the great mysteries of life is why on earth do so many of us wait so very long to lay claim to God's gifts?

Marie T. Freeman

Slowly and surely, we learn the great secret of life, which is to know God.

Oswald Chambers

The damage done to us on this earth will never find its way into that safe city. We can relax, we can rest, and though some of us can hardly imagine it, we can prepare to feel safe and secure for all of eternity.

Bill Hybels

Turn your life over to Christ today, and your life will never be the same.

Billy Graham

GATHER YOUR THOUGHTS
Write Down at Least Three Things That Your Daughter Needs to Hear from You About Eternal Life

_____

_____

_____

_____

_____

_____

_____

_____

_____

_____

_____

_____

_____

_____

More Wisdom
from Mom

On the following pages, jot down any
additional lessons, stories, or insights that
you wish to share with your daughter.